T0006640

PENGUIN BUSINESS
UNFILTERED

Ana Lueneburger has had a global career with organizations such as
INSEAD, Danone and the Boston Consulting Group. Following a decade
and a half of coaching and advisory work, Ana is a Master Certified Coach
(MCC) with the International Coaching Federation, has a PhD in business
from the University of St Gallen, Switzerland, was a postdoctoral research
fellow in change management at INSEAD, France, and a founding fellow
of the Institute of Coaching at Harvard Medical School, USA. Ana is also a
fully licensed and accredited integrative psychotherapist in the UK.

Saurabh Mukherjea works for Marcellus Investment Managers and is
the bestselling author of *The Unusual Billionaires, Coffee Can Investing:
The Low-Risk Road to Stupendous Wealth* and *Diamonds in the Dust:
Consistent Compounding for Extraordinary Wealth Creation*. A London
School of Economics alumnus, Saurabh is also the founder–director of the
Association of Portfolio Managers in India, a CFA charterholder and a
fellow of the Royal Society of Arts.

ADVANCE PRAISE FOR THE BOOK

'Coaching (from a client's perspective) is neither a magic bullet nor a one-time event. It is a path towards self-discovery and becoming a better version of yourself which you can choose to walk on or not. This book serves as an excellent and rich guide on this path'—**Marc Bitzer**, chairman and CEO, Whirlpool Corporation

'I remember the psychoanalyst Anthony Storr once saying that "originality implies being bold enough to go beyond accepted norms". The book written by Ana Lueneburger and Saurabh Mukherjea passes this test. I am happy to say so because, as an early pioneer in the coaching domain, far too many coaching books are passing my desk. Unfortunately, too many of them give me a sense of déjà vu. In comparison, it is nice to encounter a very different book that's not only truly engaging but gives the reader an in-depth view of the coaching experience. Reading this book will be a great journey, providing a wealth of insights. What's more, it may influence you more than you think'—**Manfred F.R. Kets de Vries**, Distinguished Clinical Professor of Leadership Development and Organizational Change, the Raoul de Vitry d'Avaucourt Chaired Professor of Leadership Development, and Emeritus, INSEAD, France and Singapore

'To me, human resources is the true partnership between people and business—and coaching is a powerful element of our practice. What struck me most about *Unfiltered: The CEO and the Coach* was the examination of executive coaching as a partnership—a partnership that requires both sides to have an open mind and a willingness to grow. Further, Lueneburger and Mukherjea offer alternating narratives, which makes for an interesting read for any professional (HR or otherwise) who has ever wished they could read a colleague's mind! I'm a firm believer in coaches helping to drive change and inspire leaders to be more effective—and know that seasoned and newer coaches alike will surely benefit from reading this book'—**Paige Ross**, PhD and global head, human resources, Blackstone

'This work by Ana Lueneburger and Saurabh Mukherjea is a welcome addition to the body of work on leadership for anyone looking to raise their level of effectiveness through executive coaching. By exploring the art and science that make up the alchemy of a successful coaching relationship, this original work demystifies the process and experience of the coaching collaboration from both the coach and client perspective, and the catalytic outcomes that can be expected as a result. I have been the direct beneficiary of remarkable coaching experiences throughout my career (on both sides of the equation), and finally, there is a guide for those looking to identify and maximize the impact of one of the most intimate and meaningful relationships in their professional life. I wish I had it as a handbook at the start of my career!'—**Matt Goldberg**, president and CEO, Tripadvisor

'*Unfiltered*'s refreshingly candid narrative, by Saurabh Mukherjea, a business CEO, and Ana Lueneburger, his coach, offers a unique window into the somewhat mysterious world of executive coaching. By sharing their real-life process, this book delivers an insider's perspective on the power of coaching, what it feels like to be coached and the elements that are critical to the success of this partnership. An invaluable guide for any leader who is managing growth and complexity in a rapidly evolving business environment'—**Matt Reintjes**, CEO, YETI

'A must-read! There are still too many command-and-control leaders who will profit from this fresh, insightful book. The average manager and coach too will gain from this insider's best-practice guide from both sides of the table. And so, in fact, will any reader who wishes to cultivate curiosity and lightness. I used to believe that management GURU stood for "Good at Understanding but Relatively Useless". But after reading this, I've changed my mind'—**Gurcharan Das**, author of *India Unbound, The Difficulty of Being Good: On the Subtle Art of Dharma* and *Kama: The Riddle of Desire*, former CEO, Procter & Gamble India, and former managing director, Procter & Gamble Worldwide (Strategic Planning)

'The concept of an executive coach for CEOs was not something that was widely known when I actively ran my company as the managing director many years ago. But having read this interesting book by Saurabh and his coach Ana Lueneburger, I feel there could have been occasions when I could have benefited from an outside counsel. The real-life examples make the book all the more compelling. People in corporate leadership positions will find it very useful'—**Narotam Sekhsaria**, author of *The Ambuja Story: How a Group of Ordinary Men Created an Extraordinary Company*, chairman emeritus, Ambuja Cements Limited, and chairman, Narotam Sekhsaria Foundation

'A leader has to constantly grapple with difficult judgement calls. If you are looking to understand how coaches help leaders navigate personal and professional challenges, this book is a must-read'—**Vinati Saraf Mutreja**, CEO and managing director, Vinati Organics

'Gurus come into our lives in myriad fashions and make them richer and more meaningful. Sometimes they are parents or teachers, sometimes friends or even competitors. Perhaps they are the experiences we have in our quotidian life that teach us valuable lessons. But to learn, we must first be open; almost make ourselves vulnerable to accepting that we need to change and evolve. Ana and Saurabh have presented a definitive book on the coach-and-leader equation through a candid reflection of their personal journey. This book is a must-read if you want to appreciate the value of coaching and figure out how to maximize your own learning as a mentee!'—**Apurva Purohit**, co-founder, Aazol Ventures, and former CEO, Music Broadcast Ltd (Radio City)

UNFILTERED

THE CEO AND THE COACH

•

ANA
LUENEBURGER
and
SAURABH
MUKHERJEA

BUSINESS

An imprint of Penguin Random House

PENGUIN BUSINESS

USA | Canada | UK | Ireland | Australia
New Zealand | India | South Africa | China

Penguin Business is part of the Penguin Random House group of companies
whose addresses can be found at global.penguinrandomhouse.com

Published by Penguin Random House India Pvt. Ltd
4th Floor, Capital Tower 1, MG Road,
Gurugram 122 002, Haryana, India

Penguin
Random House
India

First published in Penguin Business by Penguin Random House India 2023

Copyright © Ana Lueneburger and Marcellus Investment Managers 2023

ISBN 9780143461494

Typeset in Adobe Caslon Pro by Manipal Technologies Limited, Manipal

www.penguin.co.in

To Curiosity and Kindness; much like Dory and Marlin in Finding Nemo, *these two bring out the best in each other.*

—Ana

To Jeet and Malini, for helping me understand that a day without having fun is a day wasted.

—Saurabh

Contents

Foreword

This book is the right book for right now. Our multifaceted and complex world is more than challenging. Leading in this environment is extremely demanding. Understanding different opinions, values, cultures and personalities around you, including your own, is vital to being effective and thriving as a leader. Not to mention that the world and people are highly interconnected, making the understanding of trigger- and tipping-points a vital skill and competence in everyone's toolbox.

Knowing and leading yourself is a must to leading others and mastering all those current challenges. Executives in their careers are confronted with several inflection points. This causes unease, a sense of urgency to up your game, a necessity to assess your known approaches and routines, and to look in the mirror and start the important process of self-discovery. Even seasoned leaders who yielded great results in the past have to go into themselves to be able to solve new problems, in the present and in the future.

Leaders often struggle to examine and understand what is holding them back. Many are preoccupied with building a career, being promoted and facing the demands of having to come up with the right answers. This is precisely the moment to ask the right questions. Ana Lueneburger, a masterful, experienced coach, understands how to cultivate deep, trusting relationships with her clients. This, in turn, allows her to pose those vital and often challenging questions that her clients deserve to pay attention to. In *Unfiltered*, through the example of her client Saurabh Mukherjea, a high-potential leader, the reader gains an insider's perspective into that very work. Ana encourages Saurabh through her questions to effectively gather information, to question assumptions and to gain clarity. It is in Saurabh's answers that he grasps fully what he is grappling with and how he can begin to cope with different challenges. It is where he begins to thrive as a leader and an individual.

Intelligent and analytical people like Saurabh are sometimes hindered by that very intelligence and rigour from being able to recognize their own limitations. Subsequently, despite a commitment to excellence, they struggle with the important process of adequately reviewing and rethinking their thought processes. Strong leadership requires the agility to unlearn unhelpful behaviours and mindsets and to adopt new ones. As illustrated in *Unfiltered*, you need at least an equal but different intelligence (Ana) to trigger Saurabh to choose bravery over the comfort of the familiar. Together, Ana and Saurabh go beyond the visible, beyond the symptoms—they dive below the surface and go from 2D to 3D. In a search for root causes, they look at problems from different angles and how to ultimately overcome them for good.

By gently directing you towards exploring and perceiving yourself with different eyes, coaches make you aware of internal blockages and ineffective habits. Ana's coaching skills found a way around the obvious natural resistance and Saurabh's avoidance of going deeper beyond what was comfortable for him. Valuable insights that Ana so professionally brought up to the surface made Saurabh understand himself and others better. It gave him the opportunity to grow and develop as an individual. It made him better connected to himself, his team and the world around him. Vital for this remarkable transformation were Saurabh's openness, his willingness to be vulnerable and his readiness for candid self-discovery. Another final great outcome of the partnership between leader and coach was Saurabh's newly learnt capacity of asking better questions on his own. This undoubtedly will make him more equipped to successfully manage challenges in the future.

For all the Anas and Saurabhs out there who see the need of thinking more fundamentally about what they need to be successful, this book is a must-read. Current and future leaders need to come up with better answers. The way to find them is to get inspired by asking better and different questions. You will find them here.

Bram Schot
Professor of Practice, SDA Bocconi School of Management
Non-executive board member, Shell plc and Signify NV
Senior adviser, Carlyle Group
Former CEO of Audi AG and board member of VW Group

Preface

If you are interested in this book, it is likely that you want to learn about the experiences, both uplifting and challenging, of a coach and her client throughout their professional partnership. It is a book that tells both sides of their story, with the chapters alternately providing the coach and client's points of view and their joint views.

Or, possibly, your curiosity was tickled about getting a sneak peek into what customarily remains inaccessible: the highly confidential coach-client conversations. To the best of our knowledge, the coaching relationship, explored in this way from both sides of the figurative 'boardroom desk', has not been written about in a book before. That might surprise you, given the stratospheric rise in the popularity of coaching over the last couple of decades, as well as the enduring difficulties that clients frequently face in choosing the right coach. With so many coaches out there, how can anyone distinguish between them? Does employing a coach really help leaders become more effective in their jobs? And does coaching hold its promise of lasting, positive change?

That there exists no other book capturing the coach-client relationship as presented here is even more remarkable considering how keen coaches are to learn from their peers. It is in the nature of a coach to want to know more about the various mechanisms at work behind their clients' response to their approach and how they can better facilitate change. Are coaches really left to their own devices after receiving their initial professional training?

The reason no one has written a book on this topic seems to be relatively straightforward: the nature of leadership coaching is highly confidential. The sensitivity of the issues that executives discuss with their coaches makes it hard to open the doors and pull back the curtains to reveal the process of executive coaching. This is not only because it involves private, sensitive information, but also because executives are often public figures who would rather avoid public revelation of their 'improvement'. These difficulties are compounded by the reluctance of many coaches to share their personal, hard-earned development secrets, let alone their own shortcomings and self-doubts. Considering all this, it is not that surprising that such a book on executive coaching has not yet been published.

As co-authors, we are striking out to change this. We plan to go against the tide by sharing our individual narratives as leader and coach and disclosing our development through our professional partnership. By providing both sides of the 'story', we hope to offer a well-rounded account of the coaching partnership. Above all, we are keen to ensure that readers understand that executive coaching is a *partnership*, and that only by studying both versions of the 'story' can we truly appreciate the multiple layers of analysis that make for effective coaching.

How to read this book

To make this book useful to our readers, we have had to be open and honest. Laying bare our confidential conversations and inner dialogues required us to be brave. Courage is also a necessary ingredient in any impactful coaching engagement, both for the coach and the client. Throughout, we have been keen to safeguard the integrity of this book and preserve our individual perceptions. Therefore, we each first wrote down our respective stories and then only shared them with each other.

If you are already familiar with the world of coaching and are keen to immerse yourself in a coaching dialogue, we suggest you start with Chapter 6 and then explore the other parts of our journey that may interest you.

Chapter 1—Spilling the Beans is where Ana Lueneburger candidly shares from her own coaching practice of partnering with the C-suite. It covers when and why one might choose to partner with a coach. It explores several key questions that readers should ask when trying to find the right coach. It also gives readers some critical methods to apply when it comes to choosing between coaches and what such an investment may require, both in terms of time and resource commitments. Finally, the much-debated conundrum of how to measure coaching success, both *in situ* and over time, is discussed. It is essentially an industry insider's 'best practice' guide to maximize coaching impact—and is of interest to anyone in search of becoming the best version of themselves.

Chapter 2—In a Nutshell: The Coach's Perspective details Ana's impression of events in the run-up to, during and after her coaching engagement with Saurabh. As his coach, she transparently shares her lived experience, her insights as well as her critiques on how she felt and acted during her work with Saurabh, how she overcame professional obstacles and what happened throughout the coaching engagement.

Chapter 3—In a Nutshell: The Client's Perspective presents Saurabh's version of the same matters. It details his thoughts and emotions about starting with a coach, how Ana's coaching impacted his thoughts about work (and life), and to what degree the experience shaped and transformed his professional life and general outlook. Throughout, Saurabh applies his commitment to radical candour, offering the reader unprecedented insights into the client's viewpoint, alongside some very personal details. While there are, of course, common points in the client and coach versions, their differing experiences of the same events led to surprise, new learnings and sometimes, laughter.

Chapter 4—A Leader's Hard-Won Lessons reveals the key learnings Saurabh has gained over the past five years. It explains how he utilizes his coaching sessions with Ana and the readings that she shares with him as a springboard for opening up new mental pathways and new ways of doing things. As it isn't always easy to define what *is* and *is not* important, this chapter explores how readers can ask themselves and their colleagues the right questions, emphasizing the importance of questioning and investigating over answering and solving. Finally, in a broader sense, this chapter explores how, through 'servant leadership', leaders may make their teams more productive and successful.

Chapter 5—Do We Ever Arrive? is about how, in our personal development journey, we have the power and capacity to change. As change does not occur in a vacuum, Saurabh's colleagues, friends and family offer some 'data' and perspectives on the changes in Saurabh resulting from the coaching and over time. We share Saurabh's 2017 and 2021 personal results in a globally used strengths-based assessment. Originating at the University of Pennsylvania in the US, this assessment highlights an individual's signature strengths (known as their 'strengths profile') and how these can fortify the individual's drive for positive, lasting change. Saurabh offers additional insights into his roots and how his early experiences have shaped him and contributed to what drives and motivates his change agenda today.

Chapter 6—In Session: A Coaching Conversation allows readers to be a 'fly on the wall' at one of our coaching sessions. They'll learn what goes on in a life-coaching session and also what happens in between sessions. Readers will also have unique access to *what is not being said in a coaching session*— that rich inner dialogue of coach and client that indicates why some sessions are powerful and why others may fall flat. For those interested in coaching, this chapter might also be an opportunity to discover some coaching techniques they may wish to integrate into their own practice, whether as a coaching practitioner or leaders using coaching skills.

Chapter 7—Stay Curious, My Friends is centred on reflections on the key questions we sought to answer in this book. Why did our coaching relationship work? Is there a magic sauce? How did the experience impact the environment of the coaching? Which elements of our relationship can be replicated by others? This chapter is a co-authored dialogue on our experience of writing this book, how our relationship has evolved, some of our 'aha' moments, and what remains to be explored. This chapter also inspired Saurabh to think ahead aloud, openly sharing where he sees himself going next, both professionally and personally, and how the coaching might continue to be part of his future adventures.

We sincerely hope you enjoy reading this book as much as we have enjoyed writing it. Above all, we hope this book helps you, regardless of whether you are a coach, a client, a training institution for coaching, or simply a seeker of personal development with a growth mindset.

Who might want to read this book

Anyone who enjoys learning about the many facets of human development should find some interesting nuggets here. Audiences, in particular, are leaders looking to choose the right coach; 'leaders-as-coaches' who wish to apply coaching skills for their teams; HR leaders who are keen to instil a coaching culture in their organizations; beginner coaches; training institutions as part of their pedagogical curriculum; seasoned coaches with a growth mindset interested in expanding their praxis; and coaching organizations who support the growth of the coaching industry.

Prologue

Mumbai, February 2018

As is the norm in Mumbai from November through February, it was a beautiful morning with mild conditions perfectly set for strenuous exercise. At around 6.30 a.m., as the sun rose to reveal the blue cloudless sky, Saurabh finished his forty-minute run and began the set of exercises that his physio had prescribed to help him fix his back, which had been weakened from years of sitting in meetings and on thousands of flights. As he went through his exercise routine on the dew-soaked grass, his mind lingered over the discussions he had had the day before.

The evening before, over a two-hour video call with his executive coach Ana, Saurabh had shared his thoughts and feelings regarding where his career stood. Casting his mind over Ana's subsequent questions, Saurabh recognized that Ana was seeking to ensure that he was making the decision based on his values and goals rather than an emotional hijack. Then during dinner, Saurabh and his wife, Sarbani, had mulled over the decision one more time. After narrating the mandatory bedtime story to their children, Jeet and Malini, the couple continued to discuss the matter late into the night. Finally, Sarbani brought that discussion to an end by saying, '*As long as the children's education is taken care of, I don't think we should worry about too many other things.*'

The peals of laughter of the morning walkers in the park nudged Saurabh out of his reverie back into the here and now. He walked home, showered, got dressed and then gave the kids an extra-large goodbye hug before heading off to work. As he was leaving the apartment, Sarbani said, *'Please tell me that regardless of what happens today and regardless of who says what, you will not lose your temper.'* Saurabh smiled and kissed Sarbani goodbye.

On the drive to the office, for once, the morning newspaper could not hold his attention. Saurabh stopped reading, closed his eyes and counted the numbers down in his mind from 100 to 1 while trying to visualize every number. Usually, he found that this exercise calmed him down. Today, even this mental drill was of little help as thoughts of the past decade kept flooding back. The memories were bittersweet—the team he had built, the milestones they had achieved, the books published to rave reviews and the deep relationships he had cultivated with colleagues and clients. He also thought of all the children's birthdays and sports events he had missed while on business trips, the tensions at work and the critical scrutiny of every word he uttered in the media. The smooth and the rough memories interplayed in his head that morning like waves on a choppy sea.

In the office, as Saurabh sat through the daily morning meeting, the stock pitches that he usually found engrossing were failing to engage him. He walked over to the café next door to the office where he had retreated numerous times over the past decade whenever he needed some reflection time. Finally, it was 11 a.m.

He rechecked his calendar to ensure that 11 a.m. was still the scheduled slot for the meeting that he knew would change the course of his and his family's life. Then he took the lift up to the top floor of the office building and sat down with those who had managed his career over the past decade. He felt confident in what he wanted to say—he had gone over it in his head dozens of times the night before. Coming out of the meeting, a sense of peace washed over him. As he took the stairs down to his desk, he called Sarbani to say, *'It's done.'* Then, he hit 'Send' for the email that he had prepared the night before.

Realizing that it was coming up to 6.30 a.m. in the UK, the time that his parents normally woke up, Saurabh called the +44 London phone number that he knew from his teenage years. His mum picked up. *'Maa, aami chakri chedhe diyeechi'* (translated from Bengali: Maa, I have quit my job),' said Saurabh.

So, if you are tired of the same old story

Turn some pages

I'll be here when you are ready.

From 'Roll with the Changes' (1978), REO Speedwagon

Spilling the Beans
Ana's reflections

There it was, my client Saurabh's contagious ear-to-ear smile when we met up in a Marylebone café in the summer of 2021. It had been over a year of Zoom calls during the COVID pandemic, and being in person again, I felt myself uplifted: *'How are you, Saurabh?'* He beamed and replied, *'Business is going well, the kids are with their grandparents and Sarbani and I plan to go off on a trip to the Himalayas.'*

It feels good seeing your client thrive. There is probably an element of the coach patting herself on her shoulders. After all, had I not been part of that journey of seeing Saurabh rise and thrive? The importance of fulfilling one's potential and applying it to create an inspiring future for others has occupied a good part of my mind for as long as I can remember. Happily, attending to meaning and purpose is also my job. Coaching is a thrill, both literally and figuratively. I like to call it a high-impact experience that requires clients to venture into unknown and often uncomfortable territory. It's a little like skydiving—in that finding a trustworthy and reliable partner is crucial.

You wouldn't normally jump from a plane without a trained professional to help you reach the ground safely.

We ordered two bulletproof coffees and started with some general catching-up. Then Saurabh asked the question he had asked a few times over the past two years: '*I am still wondering what you actually did to help me change to the extent I have.*' Different thoughts were flying through my head when Saurabh posed this question. Not many clients ask this question. I wondered whether he was simply being curious. Or maybe he was seeking control as part of managing uncertainty and the anxiety that this can bring? Is it the leader in him who wanted to extend insights to managing his team and multiply the benefits he had personally realized? I was certain that I would be unable to offer a definitive answer as to why he had seen a transformation in himself. I had some hypotheses, based on my experience as a coach. But it's not like coaching is a mathematical equation; the space of human change is inherently complex and messy. As these thoughts were randomly coming in, I had a ping of bad conscience. I remembered that there was still *Simple Habits for Complex Times* next to my nightstand as part of the pile of books I had yet to read. You see, coaches can get distracted too!

I was brought back to the present fast when Saurabh raised his voice, '*Let's write a book about our coaching experience!*' I could feel myself wanting to find a way to back out of this one. Saurabh was a prodigious writer and had published six books already by that time. How he could write in parallel to a taxing professional life remains a mystery. But that was also part of his challenge: he tends to pack a lot on to his plate, sometimes to his own detriment. So, ironically, achieving a greater work-life balance was still something we were working on.

'*We could review our work together and see if taking a closer look at it will offer greater clarity as to what works and what doesn't and whether there is anything that might be useful for others,*' he added. I could feel that now he had me. I had previously rejected any opportunity to write a book. Writing my doctoral thesis had been such a lonely process. And I had never found a topic I was passionate enough about to write an entire book on. Maybe it is a bit like getting a tattoo: why do it if you are not 100 per cent sure you want to look at it for the rest of your life?

But Saurabh's idea reminded me of one of my favourite books by psychiatrist Irvin Yalom—*Every Day Gets a Little Closer*.[1] This book captures the journey of a therapist and his client. Independently of each other, both parties reflect on their experiences following each therapy session. At its heart, the book lays out how an overall positive outcome is possible despite the therapist and client having quite different takes on the same session or interventions. Might that be something we could replicate in some form for the coaching world?

I felt myself becoming more and more intrigued by the idea of writing such a book with Saurabh. Beyond our possibly selfish quest to answer the question as to why our coaching partnership had worked, the idea of such reflections being useful to a broader audience was appealing.

It's all already 'in there'

As a high schooler on a class trip, I was strolling through the Galleria dell'Accademia,[2] when we stumbled upon Michelangelo Buonarroti's sculpture, the *Atlas Slave*. Our local guide told us that it is one of several incomplete masterpieces in the Prisoners sculpture series, originally destined to mark the tomb of Pope Julius II.

The artist famously believed that his sculptures already existed within the stone, and that his job was simply to chisel away the excess and let the art emerge in all its glory. For me, gazing up at the 2.77 metre-tall sculpture was the first time I felt I could fully comprehend this idea.

Exhibit 1: The Atlas Slave

Source: https://commons.wikimedia.org/wiki/File:Atlas_
Slave_by_Michelangelo-Galleria_dell%27Accademia.jpg

Decades later, as I began to immerse myself in the world of coaching, I was reminded of that visual. Just like a sculpture waiting for Michelangelo to bring it to light, the real self of the client is uncovered with the help of the coach, revealing strengths, blind spots and hopes that had previously lain hidden.[3]

The central tenets of coaching are: (1) to support the clients; and (2) to challenge them so that they can reach their goals in a much shorter time than if they tackled them alone. For coaching to work, coaches and clients must contribute as equal partners in the process. Clients provide the material. Coaches, while chiselling away at their clients with their questions, offer them their undivided attention, experience and, where appropriate, advice. Strong coaching enhances a leader's personal and professional effectiveness and well-being. Often, it directly changes a leader's life, and when it does, it can indirectly impact many other lives.

Nevertheless, jumping into the blue with a single person won't come easily to every client. In my former career as an executive, I had been tasked with leading a transformational change initiative with a team that was reluctant to embrace that very change. Meanwhile, the board and my boss were pushing me to move faster. After several months, the sense of urgency from the board and the resistance from my team left me feeling supremely stuck. The stress began to manifest itself in physical symptoms, and when I got tingling shins and blisters on my tongue, I knew I needed help. I asked for an executive coach.

The board was supportive, but as they had never worked with coaches, I was tasked with picking one myself. I googled 'executive coaches' in the area and chose one that seemed to have solid credentials. And this coach was supportive and provided me access to useful resources. Leaders do not need to reinvent the wheel for the many skills they need, be it effective communication, team-building and motivation, or boosting the team's confidence and becoming a positive presence. They often need support with unlocking these skills. This was certainly true for me, and this is where the coaching was invaluable. By interviewing my team, my coach also helped me uncover blind spots about myself; the most important of them being that my drive to deliver results had turned me into a taskmaster for my team. Generally, many leaders are at a loss as to whom to confide in as they rise through the ranks. Having a coach by my side provided me with the much-needed sense of no longer 'going it alone'.

This was my first-ever coaching experience. No manual or guidance could help me learn how to hire the right coach; getting the right coach takes a degree of sound understanding of what coaching can offer and what one should be interviewing for. Even though my coach helped me visualize the problems in my work relationships, in hindsight I can see that we were not a match. Mostly, her coaching felt to me like she was following a 'formula' or programme of running monthly sessions, getting feedback and offering me tools. Looking back, I think I was looking for some more advice and guidance on how to lead my team and some insights from her into my personal derailers. I wonder how much more impactful my coaching might have been had I chosen someone else.

When coaching works well with clients, not surprisingly, it has to do with partnership. It may be a shared interest between the coach and client such as introducing cutting-edge insights from neuroscience and psychology into the work. It could be a shared sense of the love of learning. Working with a client eager to dive into the resources I provide and discuss the material proves to be also energizing for me—a win-win scenario.

Finding the right coach

Finding your match can make the difference between your coaching being an acceptable experience and a profound one. Not unlike at a professional matchmaking service, it can be helpful to interview several coaches before settling on 'the one'.[4] Generally, I recommend interviewing two or three coaches that, on paper, meet the key selection criteria for you. Interviewing more risks creating overwhelm and indecision. Experienced coaches will, likewise, make their decision about whether to take you on or not, as they too will want to feel that there is chemistry and that together you can deliver excellence.

To choose the right coach, it is key to get curious. Ask yourself and your prospective hire some good, tough questions. I have curated some sample questions for you in the Resources section in Appendix 1. You'll also find there a checklist and 'desirable' job specs, which you can tick off as you make your decision.

But first, should you hire a coach?

It is wise to start here and ask yourself if you need a coach. My personal belief is that if you can enlist a professional to help you achieve your goals, you have little reason to stop yourself. Support can accelerate development, personally and professionally. It can help you to expand your horizons, adopt a growth mindset, and get from 'A' to 'B' faster than you might be able to on your own—or even sometimes realize your passion lies at 'C' instead.

Good coaching, in short, allows you to show up as a better version of yourself. Working with a coach is a vital investment in a leader's potential. If you are in a good place, if you are strong and resilient, then you can positively impact those around you. However, you will need to invest time and resources into this process, so it is worth reflecting on this before you hire a coach.

And, are you looking for the right kind of coach?

Many types of coaching are available. Among others, they include career coaching, life coaching, wellness coaching, relationship coaching and wealth coaching. Different coaches can help us at different points in our lives and for different needs. At the time of writing, I have a coach supervisor and a peer coach and, outside of work, I have a yoga and meditation coach who has helped me feel grounded and alive. They have all been essential to my work and life. And had I not been able to draw on my own 'appreciative inquiry' and general coaching skills, I am convinced that my daughter and I would have a very different and far less resilient relationship today.

When we discuss coaching in this book, we refer to executive coaching, which is when a coach partners with individual business executives to help them optimize their leadership performance and unleash their full potential, with the aim of benefiting them, their teams and the organization. This type of coaching promises to enhance a leader's personal and professional effectiveness as well as his or her overall well-being. Sometimes, it can open a whole new perspective and change a leader's life for good.

Coaching has a global presence, though most coaches are still based in North America and western Europe. The coaching industry is booming; it has increased steadily, and when I searched for coaches on LinkedIn in March 2022, the platform returned over 6,00,000 hits. This surge in coaching is likely in part due to the complex, hybrid business environment of today, which has contributed to the demand for executive coaching and the low barriers to becoming a coach, which has increased supply.

However, this supply meeting demand has created a 'Wild West' of coaching. Executive coaching is currently an unregulated industry. Anyone can call themselves a coach and over 500 entities certify coaches worldwide. As a result, coaching has become an industry with hugely varying quality standards, which can make it a nightmare for prospective clients to find the right match.[5]

Three ingredients to finding a coach you will love to work with

Trust is a vital deciding factor in a field so unregulated and with so much choice. Most people don't trust easily. To achieve success, senior executives must swim through shark-filled waters, and so they, understandably, struggle more with trusting others.

Three ingredients are necessary to build trust—credibility, integrity and intimacy—and as the steward of the relationship, the coach will need to lead this process of building trust:

1. Credibility: The coach is qualified
2. (Motivational) Integrity: The coach and client are all in
3. Intimacy: There is chemistry between the coach and the client[6]

1. Credibility: The coach is qualified

A coach's experience, education and training enable clients to run a preliminary quality check and assess whether the coach possesses the right profile 'on paper' to work on a particular goal. These parameters can alleviate some of the concerns that come from making such a significant investment, therefore helping to foster trust.

Discerning a coach's qualifications

I was born in Germany into a culture that highly values formal education. Frequently, degrees and titles indicate that someone is serious about their field and knows what she is talking about. I have personally benefited from the upfront credibility that my doctorate grants me. Credentials from respected institutions like the International Coaching Federation (ICF) can also be considered hallmarks of a coach's capabilities. The ICF awards a Master Certified Coach (MCC) credential to around 4 per cent of all coaches worldwide.[7]

And yet, the value that individuals attribute to degrees will be subjective, depending on their background, culture and beliefs. Assumptions about credentials can also be misleading if relied on too closely. The facet of my doctorate that I have found most applicable to my work was not necessarily the content but the determination to persevere and be rigorous in my approach, looking for data and facts and applying them in my practice. I feel that curiosity and the joy of learning can be more important than other factors, as they so often feed into my work with clients. I trust that even though my doctorate opened this world for me, many other coaches who don't have a doctorate title will also share this sentiment.

'Relevant qualifications' won't always mean 'business degree'

My training and work as a psychotherapist have been incredibly valuable throughout my coaching career. I won't shy away from helping my clients process difficult emotions. We can address the root causes to drive sound, sustainable transformation. I don't believe this would be possible had I not received formal training in psychology and psychotherapy. A coach's work always considers the client's well-being, so qualifications in the human condition can greatly help this process.

The professional (and personal) experience a coach has

Perhaps you don't feel that practice should be weighted so heavily and that much more is to be said for careful study and understanding of theory. Of course, the study of theory is necessary, but I argue that life can only be truly understood once we have experienced it. When I was twenty-four, a partner at a global advisory firm told me, *'A good coach ideally has also had some good life crises under their belt before they come to coaching.'* At the time, I couldn't relate to this statement. However, after having a near-death experience in my twenties, having seen my toddler daughter come down with sepsis and fighting for her life in the ICU, and having failed to motivate my team as a young leader, I now feel otherwise. Hardships at work and in my personal life have helped me in coaching and in understanding my clients' challenges. I can confirm that they have given me a much more nuanced perspective and keener empathy when it comes to helping clients navigate their challenges that call for an understanding beyond what formal education has prepared me for.

Some coaches may feel differently about this, but I believe that while accreditation is important, more weightage should be given to professional experience. It helps if the coach has already been through the process of corporate life. The challenges I encountered while working in the corporate world became essential to my later practice as a coach. I had to bring together and motivate a new team, work with an inspirational boss and survive a bad one, navigate conflicts with peers and organizational politics, work in cross-cultural spaces and try to keep a work-life balance as a young parent. In short, I went through the essentials of surviving (and thriving) in the corporate world—something they don't teach you in business school!

Don't be fooled by appearances

A polished appearance, a fancy website and social media profile are, in my experience, noise, not signal. I advise against giving too much importance to whether or not a coach has written a book(!) or frequently speaks at events. While these achievements are not to be held against anyone, they could end up being counterproductive. I have rarely met someone who likes to hear themselves talk and be an engaged listener as well.

2. Motivational integrity: The coach and client are all in

In *Give and Take*, organizational psychologist Adam Grant describes the incredible energy inherent to being a giver without expecting anything in return.[8] Of course, a coach's fees are rarely insignificant, yet I also see significant generosity coming from my peers when it comes to going above and beyond for clients. Coaching is, for most of us coaches, a vocation, a calling. This mostly grey-haired bunch feels strongly about wanting to give back some of the hard-won lessons they have learnt in their lives.[9] Many of my colleagues in the coaching industry can look back on successful corporate careers and have impressive credentials. They are former pharmacists, military commanders, lawyers, members of executive committees in Fortune 100 companies, opera singers and entrepreneurs from various fields.

Finding out what gets your coach out of bed in the morning is a great way to learn how connected she is to coaching and, therefore, how dedicated she will be to your improvement. A coach will have her own motivations for taking on an engagement (or turning it down)—and these motivations must go beyond financial reward.

Why does your coach want to coach?

Explorative questions like this allow a potential client to gauge if the coach's motivation to coach matches the requirements of the engagement. It can also help protect clients from coaches with motivations that don't gel with their own. I suggest looking for coaches who love to keep learning. Coaching is one of the few professions that encourage extracurricular learning, so find out what investments a coach has made in his own growth and development *alongside* his practice. Has he tried to explore new territories? Remember: a coach can only go as deep with the client as they have gone themselves.

Is your coach motivated to design a bespoke experience for you?

Coaching engagements can take various structures; there is no 'one size fits all' approach. Clients should try to learn the breadth of their prospective coach's approach. The psychometrics that a coach uses could be an insight into his approach (personally I am a big believer in the Hogan instruments[10]) as well as the length of the typical coaching engagement (initially I like to set up a six-month time horizon, and then the client and I decide together whether it is time to close out the engagement or to set up additional months of coaching), the protocol he follows and the 360-degree feedback approach he uses.

Coach or couch: How deep are you willing to go?

Before I qualified as a psychotherapist, I had always looked up to my colleagues with a psychotherapy background with awe and wonder. For most coaching engagements with top executives to be transformative, the coach will need to run a 'root cause analysis' on undesirable leadership behaviour. Personal issues from the client's private life frequently come out in these sessions: when hired, less than 5 per cent of executive coaches get asked to work with a leader on non-work-related issues. Yet, for most leaders, work and life issues are closely intertwined. Unsurprisingly, almost 80 per cent of coaches end up supporting leaders in their personal challenges.[11]

I find transformational change engagements to be the most interesting and rewarding type of work. I won't accept mandates that focus solely on skills development or change at the behavioural level, and I believe that going deep is the only way to ensure that change will be meaningful beyond the short term. If a client wants to resolve her lack of self-confidence but the coach can't help her understand the underlying reasons for her inner critic, then the attempted change is unlikely to stick.

Nevertheless, if you're unwilling to wade into uncharted territory, make sure you find a coach who is respectful of this. I once worked with a coach who tried to therapize his CEO client, even though he was not a trained clinician. The CEO was so upset that I received a call from the chairman of the board, who asked me to intervene and have my colleague change his approach. It is understandable to be curious about why a client might not want to be therapized, but client boundaries must be respected.

Does your coach have his or her own coach?

This is a fair question to ask a coach, as it is common practice for coaches to have a coach supervisor. For a coach, this allows for reflective dialogues in a confidential space with another, often more senior, coach. During supervision, a coach can present a tricky coaching case to the supervisor so that the coach can find a way forward, which, in turn, helps the client to move forward. To ensure client confidentiality, in best practice, no personal data is revealed that might allow the coach supervisor to identify the client.

Individuals who become coaches without doing the heavy lifting of working on themselves are a risk to the profession, to clients and, frankly, to themselves. It is a privilege to be invited into our clients' worlds, and with that privilege comes responsibility. As coaches, we must examine and reflect on our behaviours, adjusting them where necessary. We cannot remain strangers to ourselves. What are the themes and patterns in our inner theatres? What are our hopes, desires and fears?

What other emotions do we feel? How do they impact our interpersonal relationships?

Supervision, in my experience, makes coaches better.[12] I have had a supervisor since the start of my coaching and advisory practice in 2008 and have found it to be a huge help. The supervisor challenges me to recognize my failures, not to brush over gaps in judgement, and to grow and expand my coaching repertoire. I am also a supervisor to other coaches, where I help my supervisees benchmark against best practices, provide resources if they need them and work through ethical dilemmas.

Ask yourself if you are motivated

When the leader initiates coaching, it can often indicate that he or she is self-motivated and ready for the work, but make sure that you are honest with yourself about *why* you reached out to a coach. That being said, low motivation at the outset won't always mean it will remain low. A coach can help you explore intrinsic motivators, i.e., what do you need to become more engaged?

I often work on more than one goal with a client, and this approach is common in the coaching profession. The official goal is often driven by stakeholders like the board or HR, while unofficial goals can go deeper and speak to the mind *and* heart of the client. Ideally, to see synergy effects, there has to be some alignment between the extrinsic and intrinsic goals.

A client's early hesitation can and often does change over time and they can become fully invested in the work. In my opinion, a contributing factor to this shift in motivation is that we make sure to address a client's personal needs. And even those needs may evolve throughout an engagement. A good coach will 'take a client's pulse' regularly and reassess where motivation levels are set.

Learning your values and strengths can help your coach understand your intrinsic needs. Take my client Solveig's quest to become a more composed leader. I focused on understanding what made her explode in the first place, what she cares about at a fundamental level and how that aligns with her leadership aspirations. I then worked to understand any of her needs that were left unmet at work and how meeting those needs might help her to be more satisfied at work and effective as a leader.

Clients must also accept that there will likely remain an element of 'unknowability' as part of their coaching experience. From the outset, you will not know whether this will work, whether you will indeed accomplish what you wish to achieve and also how you will emerge once the coaching is completed. There is a need to trust the process and go through the experience. Learning to accept this is important. The deep unknown is scary, and yet it can also offer an important opportunity to grow as you learn to confront it.[13]

3. Intimacy: There is chemistry between the coach and the client

As with any therapeutic relationship, the relationship between coach and client is essential to success.[14] After your first analytic screening of the coaches you interviewed, ask yourself: in your gut, which coach feels right to you?

This choice will come easier to some than to others. I was recently introduced to Tom, a senior partner at an asset management firm.[15] A Stanford MBA with a stellar, upward career in the firm, this highly analytical leader approached our first conversation like a formal job interview. After some time, I asked him how he felt about being vulnerable to another person. He seemed unfazed. I shared with him details about my cardiac arrest in my twenties, a wake-up call that had catapulted me into a very different life trajectory and led me to become a coach. Our conversation took a noticeable turn. His poker face dissolved, and he began to open up. At the end of our conversation, I thanked him for his time and suggested that he reflect on whether he would like us to work together. He looked at me for a split second and declared, '*I know already that I want to work with you.*'

That was quite the gut reaction! When I asked him what made him decide so quickly, he said, '*I get a sense that I can trust you. You feel real, and I appreciate how transparent and open you have been on this call. This is exactly what I need.*'

The keywords here are 'real', 'trust' and 'transparent'. In my experience, all these synthesize into another word: 'authenticity'. Coaches who wish their clients to show up as their authentic selves must do likewise. And this means that coaches should be prepared to lose some mandates, simply because their authentic self is not the right match for those clients. I have seen many ineffective coaching mandates being born out of a coach eager to show up as the person they thought was desired by the client rather than as their authentic self. Unsurprisingly, those mandates did not work out.

Remember that chemistry goes both ways

Not many clients ask themselves the question: why should a coach want to work with me? All too often, clients (and quite a few coaches) assume that an inquiry implies an automatic 'yes' from the coach's side. However, to ensure the work is high-quality, a coach must also want to partner with a particular client.

Sometimes, a client will express a wish to work with me immediately after our first interaction. I won't sign a contract right away, as I feel it is important that they reflect on their choice. Be wary of coaches who blindly accept such engagements.

After every introductory meeting, I also ask myself three questions:

1. Does my gut tell me to work with this individual, and if yes, why?
2. If I sense hesitation, where is it coming from, and do I believe it can be resolved?
3. What difference do I think we might make together?

Looking at my meeting notes from an introductory call with Stan, a senior partner in a law firm, I had appreciated his openness about the areas he wanted to address in the coaching. I was impressed by his intelligence, and I was also touched by his request for help. His sharp questions during our initial call, coupled with the positive traits above, helped me to determine that he would be a great, complex client to work with and that together we could make a difference.

Is your coach oversharing?

My experience has been that the more a client can be open, the more he will get out of the experience. But what about us coaches? There are different schools of thought as to how much a coach should share about himself with clients. When I first started, I followed the view, which is also promoted by the ICF, that coaches should wall off their personal world from a client. A coaching relationship is about clients and their goals, and so a coach sharing details about himself is often frowned upon.

This approach carries real merit. Following the Socratic method, the coach asks the client probing questions to stimulate critical thinking, draw out ideas and help clarify underlying assumptions and beliefs. The most 'orthodox' form of this coaching model even demands that the coach refrains from giving any advice or offering any opinion. How often are others fully present with us, deeply listening and asking thought-provoking questions, all designed to help us move towards our goals?

My own approach has evolved. First, I offer my clients insights into the newest research and data as they emerge from fields such as neuroscience. After asking their permission, I will also share with them my perspective on any given topic where I believe they can extract value. I have increasingly begun to share personal and professional examples with my clients. The idea is that coaches learn to use themselves as another 'tool' in their quest to support the client's aspirations: the chisel that works away at the stone. The governing principle here, however, is that I will only share with my client what I judge to be helpful to them and their goals and aspirations. The coaching ideal remains intact: it is not about the coach but about the client.

How 'warm' do you need your coach to be?

Bill Campbell, the Silicon Valley coach to Apple's Steve Jobs and Google's Eric Schmidt, was known for hugging his clients.[16] With clients where we are geographically apart for most of the time, my facial expressions, tone of voice and language are essential to express warmth and create connection. Many clients draw on this and find it helpful, particularly at tough moments.

By the same token, my job as a coach is to challenge my clients' limits. Coaching is not just about a breakthrough— it is also about breaking down vulnerable barriers, exploring complex topics and going through experiments that stretch clients out of their comfort zones.[17] I have my authentic way of expressing support and challenge, and it is the client who decides if that feels right to them.

Will you enjoy working with them on a personal level?

You might also want to consider a coach's character traits. I like to see the lighter side of life, and I'm a bit of a geek in that I like to base my offerings on science and research on human behaviour and well-being as much as possible. I am also spiritual, and increasingly, I also introduce quite a bit of resilience and well-being into my practice. I will, on occasion, teach breathing methods for stress management or recommend yoga poses to help clients relax. Take care to note what your coach is like, as these character traits will very likely work their way into their approach to you.

Don't worry too much about a personality clash

It can be useful to explore how a coach feels about the world, and whether she has a particular focus or coaching philosophy. It allows clients to determine more readily whether that coach is right for them. Understandably, the knee-jerk reaction might be to look for a coach who has a similar experience profile as yourself, as someone who has walked in your shoes can be better equipped to solve your challenges. Nevertheless, this can also limit you. Two pairs of eyes looking in the same direction might generate a narrow field of vision.

Ideally, coaching should provide a new lens that helps expand a client's universe. A coach with a range of experience can sometimes be more useful to clients than one who is their carbon copy. Quite often, due to the global nature of my assignments, my clients have a different background, culture and professional profile from mine. Further, change that transports us to new territories can sometimes require us to partner with someone who can take us elsewhere. It's simple logic that if you have never seen the Himalayas but want to virtually climb a peak or two, rather than hiring someone who has worked in your industry, you would be well advised to hire an experienced Sherpa.

Only on rare occasions in my career have my client and I had similar profiles. The closest example was when I worked with the general counsel of a global technology firm. My client was German and roughly my age. We had similar education and personal trajectories. However, our perspectives on people in business were quite different. It was here, in the space of difference rather than commonality, that my client noted she had some of her most useful 'aha' moments. When we come from a place of curiosity and do not feel threatened but rather intrigued by someone's otherness, real growth can happen.

Can your coach create a safe environment?

Part of the work to tap into a client's intrinsic motivations involves my helping him feel safe. I have to offer him reasons to trust me—that I am credible, that our space is confidential and ultimately, that I am someone he wants to be open with. Trust is the *sine qua non* for a coach to be able to help clients see the change they wish to see. Remember: trust is built through credibility, integrity and intimacy.[18] Watch out for coaches who show self-serving behaviours, like trying to prolong an engagement or making you overly dependent on them.

When should you hire a coach?

Are you one of those people who feel that they want a coach but also feel that now is not the right time? There is, in my opinion, no such thing as perfect timing. When a client, let's call her Laurence, and I first met, it was not the client who saw our engagement as the right time but the board, following a management appraisal by an executive search firm. Left to her own devices, Laurence may have never felt it is the right time for a coach. And yet, a bit further into the coaching engagement, Laurence was fully committed and motivated. So, while there may be a reason to hire a coach at a certain point in time, it is not uncommon to find unconscious processes at play in determining when the time is right.

The timing might be as close to perfect as it can be:

Once you know (roughly) what you want to get out of the coaching

For Laurence, the stakes were high: the board of her erstwhile employer wanted to get their CFO succession right. Laurence had made it clear that she would leave if she were not to get a promotion. A unique talent of global pedigree with deep knowledge in her field, she was a resource the firm did not want to risk losing.

The motivation to become CFO can stimulate an engagement, but it is not, in my experience, sufficient to support transformative change. The risk is high that a client simply goes through the motions and ticks the boxes, as Laurence attempted to do. Change becomes lip service: a client shows up for meetings (sometimes not even that) and on the surface, adopts some best-practice behaviours, such as delegating more effectively, and in the end, thanks everyone but mostly remains unconvinced that she should have to change at all.

I had my work cut out with Laurence; I had to understand the reasons behind her desire for that promotion. Only by identifying what was really at stake for her could I help her move the needle. Ideally, the organizational objectives and the client's goals align. In Laurence's case, both the firm and she were aligned with the goal of growing and developing her as a leader, which made the process initially easier. Nevertheless, the goal can change over the course of the engagement. After significant work and soul searching on Laurence's part, and due to external developments, she decided to take on another role in the organization's headquarters.

The caveat is that you should remain open to the goal changing as you continue your coaching journey. As Laurence gained clarity on what it would take to go from 'A' (her current position) to 'B' (CFO), during the process, she came to realize that her actual, desirable destination was 'C' (moving back to her home country and being closer to an elderly parent).

Once all stakeholders understand what's at stake

Occasionally, I get requests marked 'urgent'. Such requests tend to come from HR, and at times of organizational crisis. These scenarios rarely make for a good coaching experience. For one, coaches are often picked based on their immediate availability rather than because they are the right fit for the client. The urgency also suggests something undisclosed: that toxic behaviours at the top need fixing and cannot be resolved by coaching alone. In extreme cases, the organization is merely using the coaching relationship to go through the motions: by hiring an external coach, they can follow protocol and avoid being sued or having to offer huge payouts to the leader they wish to let go.

Since the very beginning of my coaching business, I have refused to accept these kinds of 'penalty box coaching' mandates where clients are doomed to fail as the organization has already given up on them. It is not fair to the individual leader or to the coach. And in the long term, it is rarely beneficial for the organization. Before moving forward in these situations, my advice for both client and coach is to find out where the urgency is coming from and who is driving the agenda before proceeding.

Once you have gut-checked you're in it for the right reasons

Fortunately, hiring a coach for remedial purposes seems less common today. Coaching now tends to focus on developing the capabilities of high performers. Sometimes, these explorations yield great insights. A global investment bank's head of HR reached out to me as the bank wanted to hold on to a major contributor with a rich client portfolio but who was nevertheless stunting his team's motivation. The idea was not just to hold on to him but also to 'fix him' so that neither he nor his team would walk.

After further discussions, it became apparent that while this individual leader needed help to be more effective, the real problem was that he had a highly ineffective manager who wanted to outsource her own responsibilities to me. Happily, in this instance, she was open to feedback. We shifted gears, and she became my client instead of her direct report. Over the six months that we worked together, she stepped up to her role, which positively impacted her direct report and his team.

Should you hire an independent or internal coach?

This won't always be your call to make, but for coaching to work, I believe the coach should be impartial when it comes to the client's organization and the various stakeholders. This is difficult, if not impossible, to achieve for internal coaches.

Even external coaches actively need to manage boundaries. Coaches must protect the confidential space they create for the client. This means contracting with HR in such a way that it is clear that the coach's allegiance is with the client and that no information from the coaching sessions will be shared with HR or other managers without the client's explicit permission. Most organizations, especially those familiar with the coaching model, respect this boundary. However, I have seen attempts to cross that line.

At the same time, to be effective, the coach must connect with the client's organization and learn as much as he can about it. And while an external coach may never acquire the same insider knowledge that an internal coach might, he can learn to understand the broader context of the company in question and how its leaders work.

How much should you expect to invest?

What is a typical coaching fee? The answer can only be 'it depends'. While colleagues have generously shared with me the quantum of their fees over the years, generally speaking, there isn't much transparency about these numbers.[19] The range, however, is enormous, with hourly rates of anywhere from $200 to $3500, all the way up to $1 million+ per CEO engagement, which only a few coaches worldwide receive. Most coaches also add advisory and consulting services to their quote, which increases the rates further. A coach's average global annual revenue was reported to be $47,000 in 2019, not including advisory and consulting services. At the top end of the fee spectrum are coaches with qualifications that would easily permit them to work at premier strategy consulting firms.[20]

The fees may seem costly, but in the end, the results delivered and the advantage of a professional partner at one's side are where clients see their return on investment (ROI). This remuneration model is value-based and considers a coach's education, rigorous training, aptitude and years of leadership experience, often at an international level.

How can you measure success?

Coaches can be elusive when it comes to evaluating and communicating the results of their work. It's also not entirely easy to say for what part of a successful engagement the coach should take credit. After all, clients often do the heavy lifting. I can open doors for a client, but he or she has to decide to walk through them. In their ground-breaking work on the coaching industry, Diana Coutu and Carol Kauffman discovered that close to 90 per cent of coaches discuss their clients' progress with them, yet less than 70 per cent of coaches offer a qualitative assessment of the progress to other stakeholders in the clients' organizations.[21] Less than 30 per cent offer quantitative feedback on behavioural change. And less than 25 per cent of coaches address how coaching impacts the bottom line for the business.

Effectively, how can one accurately measure the impact of an engagement in a field like coaching, which, by its very nature, tends to produce qualitative data? It is possible to quantify some elements of behavioural change. We can document client-leaders' record of timeliness, how often they used open-ended questions during interactions with their colleagues, how much they delegated tasks or the frequency of the career development meetings they set with direct reports. Other types of quantitative data are harder to gather because those data points were not solely down to the coach. It is challenging to correlate coaching interventions with the performance of a leader and her company. Can I take credit for an effective post-merger integration shepherded by the CEO I am currently coaching? Can I assume responsibility for the rising stock price of the company?

Moreover, the corporate system is an integrative component of change. Circumstances within the system—and this means the organization in which the leader works and the team around him—will impact a leader's ability to change. Coaches rarely have influence over these variables. It is a complex challenge.

You might also wonder—who ultimately decides whether an engagement is a success? Beyond the client and the coach, the immediate manager, the board, HR and direct reports can all be stakeholders in an engagement's success, and they won't always agree. Is this where the measurement of success stops?

I was once brought in to coach Cara,[22] a CEO committed to introducing her philosophy of servant leadership[23] into an 'eat what you kill' organizational culture. She had hired me to support this change agenda, as well as to help manage her stress in carrying out this monumental task. But despite the great progress she made in strengthening her influencing skills and resilience, neither the board nor her direct reports at her original institution were ready to make the required changes to allow her to succeed. Cara ultimately decided to accept an offer from a competing institution, where their values more closely matched hers. The question is, should coaching success be measured by the change made to the company or the change made to the individual? As coaches support individuals, my impression is that the aim is to ultimately ensure the individual's well-being and improvement. Frequently, this includes the needs of the organization, sometimes it does not.

Positive signals of coaching success are when an organizational client continually calls up for more work with other leaders, when word-of-mouth leads to new work after years have passed of having partnered with a leader, or when a leader calls to continue the working relationship.

Consider how long you will want to measure results

The most powerful indicator of coaching success is when the results are maintained over time. One reliable method to achieve this is to set up milestones before, during and after the coaching relationship.[24] 'Before' can be a management appraisal report by an executive search firm and a 360-degree feedback process as well as my own impressions at the outset of an engagement. The 'during' can be multiple check-ins with various key stakeholders, such as the board, as well as *in situ* observations, such as my client's interactions with direct reports, and, of course, the client's and my reflections. The 'after' may be when I sit down with the client's key stakeholders to assess the outcome of the work. All of this often takes place in a span of six months.

It isn't always obvious at what point this third and final stage ends.[25] To date, no formal research has systematically followed coached executives over a longer period of time. There are likely good reasons for this, including the cost of tracking long-term change. Other variables would need to be considered as part of the process, such as a leader's personal circumstances (i.e., a divorce, empty-nester grief or winning the lottery) and professional circumstances (such as additional trainings, coaching engagements or change in reporting lines). And, of course, leaders move on. These variables mean that tracking long-term change may not just be complex—it may be impossible.

One measure for determining sustained change can be the length of time a leader stays connected to a coach following their contractual engagement. Sometimes, a coach will stumble across data confirming that the change did not remain. I once worked with the CEO of a successful publishing house, let's call him Ronan, who struggled with a high turnover on his team. When I ran Ronan's 360-degree feedback, the message came loud and clear: he was considered a bully, and his directs were fearful of his frequent outbursts and verbal abuse. My client was shocked when he read this report—people rarely realize the effect they have on other people. He decided to make significant changes to his behaviour: name-calling and public shaming were out, and empowerment and hands-off delegation were in. When we closed the engagement after eight months, the change was tangible: Ronan had stopped shouting at people, he had become a stronger listener, and he had offered each employee shares in the organization.

On reading this, you might think that this engagement was a success, but *was* it? A year after I had tied up the work, I received a note from Ronan's personal assistant, who had decided to resign. Instead of maintaining that change, my client had regressed to some of his old behaviours. Despite my recommendation in my final report to bring in an independent chair of the board, he had continued to hold on to that position. No one could hold him accountable except himself, and so it became easier once more to do whatever he wanted.

Without an individual leader's commitment and some form of checks and balances in place, regression to the previous status quo—or 'reversion to the mean', as investors call it—is a real danger. Initial change is not as difficult. It's often exciting to try out something new. *Sustainable* positive change is hard, and this is true even if we *want* to change. No wonder four out of five people drop their New Year resolutions by February every year.[26] I believe that a client's success in maintaining transformation even several years on is because, at least in part, he or she owns the change; and also because there are accountability mechanisms that remain in place, including regular check-ins with the coach.

I believe that, as the coaching industry matures, the call for coaches to showcase more clearly how they bring about change and offer a credible methodology for measuring impact will increase.

*

The questions in this chapter are those that I would ask as a client about my prospective coach. But this chapter wouldn't be complete without a few notes about how coaches can help themselves at this critical juncture—when a client is deciding whether to hire them. I hope my answers to the questions will also help prospective coaches understand what their clients can reasonably expect of them.

As a coach, be willing to embrace variety

Coaches would do well to move out of their comfort zone to increase their repertoire. A few months ago, I was asked to join the faculty of a black leadership programme for a prestigious global strategy consulting firm. The programme was for senior leaders in the US and the UK, and I was the only white German female on the faculty. I didn't have even nationality or culture as a common denominator with the rest.

A little voice told me to step away from this challenge, and it was quite convincing: what if these clients did not accept me, seeing as this programme was about their challenges as minorities? What if I could not offer the insights they would rightfully expect? My spirit of curiosity finally got the upper hand and, hands down, this work has been one of the most rewarding experiences in my professional career. It was thought-provoking and impactful, and it has inspired me to take more risks in other coaching engagements. Based on the feedback, it also turned out to be an advantage for the programme to have someone in the room with a different background, as it allowed them to question their own assumptions and offered a fresh perspective on the challenges they faced.

Ensure you'll make a difference by focusing on strengths

As part of my coaching certification, I took a master class with Christopher Peterson, who at the time was a professor at the University of Michigan. One of the founders of positive psychology, he has been listed by the Institute for Scientific Information (ISI) as among the 100 most frequently cited psychologists. I was inspired by Chris's humility and his wealth of knowledge. He introduced me to the link between top performance, well-being and character strengths.[27] Lyle Spencer, a world authority on talent selection and development, summarized these intersections thus: '*You can train a turkey to climb a tree. But I'd rather hire a squirrel.*' In coaching, rather than working with clients on fixing their weaknesses, we can help them identify and leverage their signature strengths. Turkeys run faster than squirrels can (and they can fly, which squirrels cannot).[28]

In business, the challenge is to ensure that the turkeys do most of the running and all the flying, while the squirrels do the climbing. When coaching business leaders, the opportunity to bring change in them lies in finding ways to enable the turkeys to run and fly faster and the squirrels to climb higher. In the chapters that follow, we discuss how playing to our strengths can help us see our learning curves, feel energized and find excellence. It was still a novel idea when I first introduced this in my coaching in 2009. As I am writing these lines, it has become a core component of my intake repertoire, and this approach is increasingly mainstream in the world of executive coaching.

The concern that we may neglect weaknesses with this approach still occasionally comes up. Yet, by focusing on strengths, we also pay attention to whether signature strengths are overplayed. Overplayed strengths are truly where leaders end up derailing (see Chapter 5). One of my top five strengths is Appreciation of Beauty and Excellence, and for me, this may show up in my admiration of a beautifully presented French pastry or of a carefully worded piece of advice from a colleague. It sounds like a wonderful strength to have. But when it is overplayed, this strength can make us hypercritical. People with this strength, if overplayed and turned inwards, tend to be their own harshest critic. Turned outwards, this criticism will extend to others when expectations are not met. I am acutely aware of this problem, having been a taskmaster for my team when I was an executive too. The art is in learning how to leverage one's strengths and not to under- *and* over-use them, as well as avoiding going around in circles by trying to rectify weaknesses.[29]

How to price yourself as a coach

Coaches are notoriously ill at ease when it comes to charging for their services. For many of us, our profession is also our vocation. How can you charge for something that you enjoy doing? What may make the process even more uncomfortable is that we are entering a transactional exchange with the party we are building a strong relationship with. A strong relationship is key when it comes to being able to support and challenge our clients. Here, it can be helpful for HR to be the sparring partner and to manage the transactional part of the relationship, i.e., setting up the contract and payment process through them. This also helps ensure that HR is familiar with the coaching process, which, in turn, will help things run more smoothly further down the line.

When I started coaching, an experienced leadership coach told me: *'Never work with individuals, only work with organizations. Individuals do not want to pay you properly and will expect miracles.'* After working with private individuals, I decided to follow his advice. My mantra has been to charge organizations fair fees, incorporating their budget and my experience in the quote. I do not believe in selling myself short or in being discounted as a single business owner for a Fortune-500 client. I also believe in giving back, as I offer reduced rates for non-profits and take on pro-bono coaching engagements for select start-ups.

When coaches should say 'no'

There can be good reasons to decide *against* working with a client. This is strongly dependent on the leaders' philosophy and whether they can accept outside support. If they are unwilling to accept this support and they cannot be persuaded by any argument, they will always see their coach as a nemesis to fight against. Circumstances like time and organizational resources also play a role. If the leaders are not able to carve out any time for their own growth and improvement, then the coaching process will only frustrate them and the coach.

*

Let's come back to that moment in the Marylebone café in the summer of 2021. Here was our opportunity, Saurabh's and mine. By the time we left that café, we, client and coach, had entered into a pact to write *Unfiltered*. We committed to be bold, to eschew norms and to open the normally inviolable doors that shield coaching conversations.

In Chapter 1 we have laid the ground for the subsequent chapters, where we address the more complex process questions about how leaders can change their mental pathways as they build their teams, their businesses and, ultimately, their careers. For clients interested in coaching we look to answer questions such as 'What does a coaching process look like?', 'What happens in a coaching session, what does it feel like?', or 'Is this an experience I want to pursue?'

For coaches who are starting out or who are interested in benchmarking their own practice, we look to answer questions such as 'What is the general journey you take with the client?', 'Where do you start with a client? With trust, with ego, language, self-awareness, vulnerability . . .?', or as granular as 'What are the activities/exercises/experiments that you ask them to do?'

Key Takeaways

- Essential ingredients for coaching success are that the coach is qualified, the client is motivated to embrace change and the chemistry between coach and client is good.
- Clients ultimately will have to trust their gut when it comes to finding the right coach. But there are some key questions clients can ask to get more clarity:

    1. When did you decide to become a coach, and what made you decide to do so?
    2. What do I need to know about you that is not on your bio?
    3. What is your coaching philosophy?
    4. How does this philosophy translate into your practice, and how do you coach in general?

5. Who do you like to work with, and why?
6. Why should I work with you?
7. What is your most treasured failure as a coach?
8. Do you have a supervisor, and how often do you see him or her?

- Clients should also understand a coach's experience and background, approach and mindset (please go to Appendix 1 in the Resources section for more details).
- Fixing weaknesses is not the answer. Coaching based on strengths is where we can identify true derailers. It is with a strengths-based focus that the difficult endeavour of change becomes energizing and sustainable.
- Coaches equally need to be selective as to which engagements they take on.

We shape our self
to fit this world

and by the world
are shaped again.

The visible
and the invisible

working together
in common cause,

to produce
the miraculous.

Excerpt from 'Working Together' by David Whyte
(David Whyte, *The House of Belonging*, Many Rivers Press, 1997.)

CHAPTER 2

In a Nutshell: The Coach's Perspective

Ana's reflections

Off to a promising start

In the spring of 2017, I received a call from a partner with a global executive search firm: *'We have a CEO succession client for an investment bank in Mumbai. He is being assigned a coach, and given the requirements of the mandate, we want to put you forward.'* I had already partnered with a number of Indian executives, mostly through my work at INSEAD's Global Leadership Centre. In my experience, Indian clients brought a contagious mix of enthusiasm and curiosity into their work, and I had much enjoyed experiencing their energy. I felt in a bit of a rut, and this seemed like a very welcome opportunity to stretch myself. *'Go for it,'* I told myself.

This client would be Saurabh Mukherjea, an Indian resident who had partly grown up in the UK. Saurabh was running the brokerage and investment management arm of the bank, and I was told he had built the business to a point where the bank had become a respected competitor to other global financial powerhouses in India. The bank had been working in institutional equities for about five years before Saurabh joined—he was the fourth CEO to be recruited to lead this arm of the business. I knew from my experience that these were often tough roles to step into, especially at the time he did, when the bank was losing ground under fierce competition from other banks. It turned out to be a Herculean effort, but I learnt that Saurabh and his team had swiftly moved the brokerage and investment management practice of the bank from the red into the black, bringing in a profit in a corporate entity accustomed to seeing red ink flow freely.

It takes real personalities to overhaul businesses like this—and to accept the challenge in the first place. Intrigued, I said yes. The executive search firm set up a videoconference chemistry call for Saurabh and me over Zoom. These 'chemistry calls' usually take about sixty minutes, but I always make sure I do not have something scheduled right after. As I opened the Zoom window, I was in a woolly sweater as London was freezing. The second window opened, and here was Saurabh, behind him a wall of books and a ceiling fan was whirring like it was about to take flight—clearly it was boiling hot where he was! *'Hi, Ana, nice to meet you.'* His smile lit up his face and a genuine warmth entered our Zoom room.

After exchanging some pleasantries, Saurabh began asking questions: *'Can you tell me a bit about your coaching approach?'* I shared a few nuggets, such as that I use a strengths-based approach where—through an assessment—we would take stock of where he sees quick learning curves and review how well he does when it comes to leveraging his strengths currently. *'How often will we meet and how much work is there between sessions?'* This is a fair question as coaching is quite an investment, not only in terms of finances but also in terms of time. But I had an inkling that he might not want to invest too much time in this 'exercise' and that Saurabh was sceptical about the idea of hiring a coach in the first place—having been in the business a long time, I can sense these things. By the same token, though, he also seemed excited about it as he certainly had many questions. It would be the first of many contradictions, and I had been briefed by the executive search firm that I was dealing with a strong personality of great depth. What also struck me was how many books he had read on human functioning and positive psychology. I had recognized some of the spines on his bookshelf—many that were also on my own. Handbooks on good communication skills. Psychological treatises. Psychiatry in theory and practice. These became great talking points during this first session, although I couldn't help but wonder: if he knew all the theory, what was he hoping to learn from *me*?

We were both aware of the obstacles of being thousands of miles apart, but Saurabh had made a positive impression on me during this initial call. When Saurabh told me that he wanted to partner up, I was nevertheless excited. Coaching, in my opinion, should be left to the professionals who have the training and education to back up their impressions of the client, but sometimes you also have to listen to your gut: I liked Saurabh as a person. I felt we could do some good and, even more importantly, *groundbreaking* work together. Saurabh would challenge me—I was certain of that even then.

The email that threw it all into chaos

The first step, we agreed, would be for me to send him a proposal. Proposals are time-intensive, but they're an important way to let both coach and client understand the general conditions of what they have agreed on, and they offer a framework and target. 'General conditions' is the operative phrase here, as proposals like these tend to be worded in a way that safeguards client-coach confidentiality. We generally don't want to get too granular at this stage. After all, HR and other organizational stakeholders will likely review it too.

As is frequently the case in six-to-eight-month coaching engagements, I had set aside the first phase for discovery and trust building, the second phase for commitment and implementing, and the third phase for reinforcing any behavioural changes that the leader identifies as well as looking ahead to set the client up for success also after the coaching engagement concludes.

Exhibit 2: An overview of the coaching process

Coaching Process, Sample Overview

Phase 1: Discovery & Trust Building	Phase 2: Commitment & Implementation	Phase 3: Reinforcement & Looking ahead
Time horizon (approx.) Month 1	**Time horizon (approx.)** Months 2 to 4	**Time horizon (approx.)** Months 5 & 6
Coach Key Objectives 1. Understand the client's values, motivations, goals and identify strengths and derailers 2. Create a coalition for change with key organizational stakeholders	**Coach Key Objectives** 1. Build a change vision together with the client 2. Facilitate the client's change agenda through being a sounding board, identifying obstacles, tackling resistance	**Coach Key Objectives** 1. Measure and reinforce progress 2. Make sure change sticks and develop a support plan for post the coaching engagement
Client Action Items *Client Intake Questionnaire *Hogan Psychometric *VIA-IS Strengths Inventory *360-degree feedback – stakeholder nomination, behavioral interviews, Confidential 360-degree Feedback Report	**Client Action Items** *Client Leadership Development Plan based on the Confidential 360-degree Feedback Report *Experiment with new behavior *Build knowledge on relevant leadership best practices *Check in with stakeholders	**Client Action Items** *Check in with stakeholders *Fine-tune goals & add new ones based on aspirations and system's feedback *Build and execute on a Personal Board of Directors

Source: Dr. Ana Lueneburger, Fox meets Owl Limited

We had also agreed that I would spend a week in Mumbai to observe him in his 'natural work environment'. I sent the proposal off without much concern—these proposals act like contracts more than anything else. Saurabh's response came quickly. It was a shock to me—normally, I expect these replies to come much later, and he was a busy man in charge of a big business. Another surprise awaited me. I opened it to find not a single sentence of acceptance as I was accustomed to receiving, but *half a page* of notes. To say he was not happy with my proposal would be an understatement. Here is a sample of what the email contained:

Dear Ana,

It was good meeting you. Thank you for sending your letter of proposal. But I must say that I am disappointed by its content. Given your experience and profile, I would have expected a more personalized version whereas this feels like a generic offer, applicable to anyone. I would suggest you take more time to fine-tune your proposal, to capture our conversation in appropriate detail and share it when it is ready. I have added comments to your proposal so you can see what I am referring to.

Thank you, Saurabh

The negative feedback was strong and chastising, and the tone pressed the notion that I should know better. I was surprised, but I was also a bit annoyed. It wasn't so much the content of Saurabh's message—over more than a decade of partnering with C-suite leaders, I was well used to dealing with people with high expectations and demands. It was that the tone was off. I felt like a truant schoolchild who had been sent to the principal's office. Often, there is an expectation, mostly held by coaches themselves, that we must be enlightened human beings who do not get flustered, even when our feathers get ruffled. But we can't put the brakes on our feelings completely. When I received Saurabh's email, I remember thinking: *Who does he think he is?* I couldn't help but feel my wounded pride. I had a full client book already! I didn't need to take on this engagement. And I had always positioned myself as a partner to clients, not as a child to be told off.

After taking one deep breath (or maybe two), I could distance myself from my initial reaction, and my curiosity kicked in again—something that I believe is an essential characteristic of a coach. Here was something interesting we could potentially use if we worked together. Was this indicative of how Saurabh communicated with his colleagues and peers? Was he aware of the impact his words made? Why would he offer feedback in such a brutal way, given that he knew so much about the principles of good communication? And maybe most important of all, why was there such a lack of curiosity as to why I would not have captured our confidential first conversation in an official document, was there maybe a reason (such as others reviewing it)?

Of course, I also wondered if he would continue the engagement with me at all; as is often the case in executive coaching, he had interviewed another coach too. This other coach was someone I knew and had a very different style from mine. Despite the possibility that Saurabh might not choose me, I jotted down some notes for a conversation I was sure would one day come. It wouldn't do to tell him these things now—I would wait my turn, when I could use it to accelerate his growth. In my work, it's always important to know when to share and when to hold back. It's a little like dancing—timing is everything.

A scholar in the suit of a CEO

Looking back, I'm not sure if I was surprised to hear that Saurabh had decided to work with me after all. We humans are beautiful in our complexity, and in that sense, Saurabh was no different. A few weeks after we had signed our contracts, Saurabh was visiting London for one leg of an extended business trip. He wanted us to meet in person. I was sipping mint tea at a Pret a Manger close to St Paul's Cathedral, wondering how this meeting might turn out. Much research has been done on the power of first impressions. We had met before via videoconference, but first in-person encounters are another matter entirely.

Saurabh entered—medium height, busy step. He was pulling a small black carry-on suitcase with wheels that seemed to growl in warning, and I sensed a restlessness in his movements even as he sat down—a physical manifestation of a racing mind. I think he ordered a strong tea, no sugar. Aside from the drink order and the guard-dog suitcase, he sat with a casual air and was dressed humbly for someone of his seniority and success. The black suit he wore was too wide for his shoulders, and underneath it, his white button-down shirt seemed to balloon, made more apparent by a narrow red tie that split him down the middle. What a difference from the well-tailored suits of fine cloth that I was used to seeing on my clients!

Saurabh wanted to get down to business immediately. He listed the people at the bank I should speak to as part of the 360-degree interview process that would help us understand his colleagues' perceptions of him. He talked about his expectations from the coaching sessions. We would start work the following month, with the goal of ending our collaboration six months from the starting date. He spoke far more than he asked questions. And in case you're wondering . . . no, we did not talk about The Email.

Talking with Saurabh felt both energizing and exhausting. As a coach, you have to take slow steps to understand a person entirely, yet with Saurabh I felt this sense of urgency, as if he always had one foot out the door. Even so, I couldn't shake the impression that in front of me was an intellectual playing at being the big business CEO. He very much wore his intellect on his sleeve!

It was only when we began walking towards my next meeting that the conversation moved away from business and became more personal. In moments on this short walk, he would flash me a big smile, and it felt like rays of sunlight coming through busy, passing clouds. Just before we parted ways, Saurabh shared some painful personal memories he had of growing up. Having arrived in the UK as an adolescent, he had felt like an 'outsider' both at home where things were tense due to tight finances and in school where he was the 'odd man out' among his British classmates. I was beginning to see the person behind the performance. There is something peculiar about the moment just before the end of a session; that's when I find my clients say what they really want to say, and that's when they talk about what's eating them up inside. Subconsciously, clients feel safe during that time window when the session is just about over because they can unload their innermost feelings while also not having to worry about these being discussed and scrutinized. These are moments that I very much treasure as a coach, as this is where the real work takes place.

As part of his homework, I emailed Saurabh my client intake questionnaire, which contains thirty questions of both professional and personal nature. There are questions one might expect such as 'Briefly describe your current responsibilities (including work hours per week, whether you primarily manage people or projects, and the number of people reporting to you)'. Then there are questions that require more introspection such as 'What complaints do you think your direct reports/peers/ supervisor have about you? How do you think they would like you to change?'. These offer a means to gauge what a leader does and how self-aware they are when it comes to their impact on others. The intake also contains questions of a more intrusive nature such as 'What do you consider your biggest personal failure?' or 'Who has influenced your choices in real life and why?'. It offers a sense as to a client's values and belief systems and, depending on the degree of candour in their response, how open they are willing to be at this early stage of the coaching.

In character, Saurabh turned the intake questionnaire around within twenty-four hours. There were moments of candour in his replies that felt promising for the journey ahead of us. To the question 'Which historical figure do you most identify with and why?', Saurabh replied, '*Winston Churchill— We will fight on the beaches, we will fight on the streets . . . we shall not give up.*' I sensed perseverance bordering on toughness. And to the question 'What keeps you up at night?', he responded, '*I worry about whether I can give the kids the life they deserve. Will their upbringing be happier than mine was? Will they be more comfortable in their skin than I am?*' To 'When you die, what would you like people to say about you?', he shared, '*He was a force for good.*' There was a degree of tenderness coupled maybe with a sense of purpose and the hope of making a difference.

Not long after Saurabh and my encounter, I met the bank's founder and CEO. This encounter was very different from my first in-person meeting with Saurabh. For one, the founder arranged to meet me in the swanky tearoom of the Ritz-Carlton in London—quite a difference from meeting at a generic sandwich chain! Short in stature, he had a commanding presence and dominated the tearoom the very moment he entered. In stark contrast to Saurabh's humble, professorial appearance, this man gave the impression of being at home in the world.

Soft-spoken and well-mannered, he showed his support for the engagement between Saurabh and me and emphasized his hopes for the outcome. I was struck by how he talked about Saurabh—much like a benevolent father might about his son. And yet, throughout this meeting, I noticed a certain guardedness. The founder left me with the distinct impression that he wasn't sharing the whole picture of Saurabh as he saw him.

There's always something they won't tell you

Once I have come to know a client, I must understand their work environment. This means interviewing the people closest to them, and this research should come early in the process to ensure that my impressions as a coach don't tilt too strongly one way or another. For us, this came a few weeks in, after I had three sessions with Saurabh. As I began interviewing key stakeholders within and outside the bank, I found several common narratives: Saurabh was bright, hardworking and a man of principle. He also had a track record of professionalism that many admired. The main areas in which they wanted him to grow were his interpersonal relationships and communication style. Interesting—again, communication and relationships were being earmarked as potential weaknesses. Likely, The Email hadn't just been a fluke. Some also expressed concern that Saurabh might not be all that passionate about becoming group CEO. I found these concerns unusual, considering how engaged Saurabh was in a coaching process where the explicit goal was to prepare him for that very role.

What surprised me the most about these interviews was that almost every rater wanted to know if his or her responses would be kept confidential. While there is always a certain level of 'angst' around giving feedback in these contexts, this was a few degrees above what I usually see. The respondents (I call them 'raters' in feedback reports) were evidently nervous about the possibility that Saurabh might know who said what, and that nervousness didn't diminish even after I reassured them that I would anonymize their quotes in the report that Saurabh would see. Why was everyone so nervous that he might connect the dots? And how honest would they dare to be?

Once all the raters had shared their feedback, I discovered that the ultimate problem area for Saurabh was going to be difficult to overcome: people were afraid of him—and everyone felt this way, all the way up to the most senior executive levels. The fear of entering a contentious space with Saurabh had made it nearly impossible even for the otherwise confident founder to communicate directly with him. He had instead hired a senior executive to shuttle messages back and forth between them. This was a pattern.

Saurabh had read the full brief prior to our session. And yet, from the moment the session started, I perceived a shift in his energy. When clients receive these feedback reports, the coaching intensifies. These are the moments when the conversation will go beyond the surface. Receiving feedback on a leader from his or her business environment is a crucial milestone for any coaching mandate. It solidifies the initial goalposts and often adds nuance and even new goals to the mix.

As for the shift I saw in Saurabh, while he had always appeared interested in our one-to-one discussions and the articles I shared with him, I had sometimes felt that he was only going through the motions of it all. But this 360-degree feedback report managed to touch him in a way our previous conversations had not. We were no longer in pretend land—we had now entered a space that felt raw and real.

My approach to sharing the 360-degree feedback is to first summarize the feedback highlighting the key strengths that emerge as well as where the client has room to develop. Then I share quotes, which I have stripped of any content that could give away who said them. I also group these quotes into themes—this, I find, facilitates the client review. Some coaches do not provide quotes in their feedback reports but, instead, share feedback in a more general fashion. In my experience, though, the risk of diluting feedback in this approach is high, as is the possibility that the recipient may overlook the seriousness of critical messages. By generalizing feedback, these reports stay at an 'above the neck' level, very much in the cerebral part of processing information, and they fail to reach the heart and gut of a client. Today, I prefer to provide the anonymized quotes first and let the clients develop their own hypothesis on the emerging themes without my guidance. Only once we have had this conversation will I hand them my summary. This has the benefit of not polluting the client's thinking and of allowing the client to stay in the driver's seat when it comes to making sense of the results. And yet, this type of giving feedback is also more demanding of the coach. It requires that a coach delicately explore the feedback with their clients to make sure they do hear what their raters are saying and don't succumb to the understandable urge to get defensive and ignore it.

When Saurabh heard that his colleagues and peers were afraid of him, he was surprised. It seemed that he was genuinely not aware of the impact his words and actions had—a busy man who was already thinking of his next meeting, he mostly acted in the moment. But something had to change. Saurabh's temper made the talent on his team reluctant to take risks and caused his peers to avoid him. While external media outlets ate up the candour and radical transparency Saurabh embodied, it was that very same candour and transparency which, when he was under pressure, exploded in the confrontational behaviour that internal stakeholders shied away from. And Saurabh was under pressure a *lot*.

We finally talk about The Email

Here was my call to be tough. This was an opportunity to really help Saurabh deepen his understanding of how his unfiltered reactions landed with others. In my experience, anything that happens in the coach-client space should be considered as valuable information to be leveraged for the benefit of a leader's development and growth. The trick is in knowing when to hold back and when to speak up. As his coach, it was in his interests that at this time, just moments after he received a great deal of anonymous feedback, I could be his 'sparring partner' who could vouch for those comments. I openly told him how his email had made me feel; that I felt a pang of unpleasant surprise in being scolded like a child. I told him that my decades of professional training and experience had let me see it as it was: a response from someone unaware of his impact, probably as harsh with himself as he was with others (if not more), and clearly under an enormous amount of pressure. But his colleagues, who didn't have that context, were likely to feel very differently.

This feedback allowed me to see his more vulnerable side to an extent that he had not shared in our previous three sessions. I felt privileged and honoured that he would trust me with his emotions so soon. '*I am shocked and hurt,*' he shared. Honest feedback is one of the true gifts we can receive in life. Yet many of us are familiar with the pain that candour of the sort Saurabh was facing at that moment can bring. The easiest way to deal with such discomfort is to dismiss it. What takes courage is to explore the truth in what has been shared with us. Only then can we take the first steps towards growth and towards becoming the best version of ourselves.

I empathized with Saurabh. Telling people hard truths is never easy, even for a qualified coach. And this was a man who went to great lengths to keep his company competitive and his colleagues effective. As far as he was concerned, he was doing everything for everyone else's 'good'. He would keep himself occupied at all hours, fly economy class across the Atlantic, take painkillers and just push through, working harder than anyone around him, all with the intention to improve quality, improve structures and improve management at his company. He firmly believed that pushing people beyond their limits was part of his leadership responsibilities. But the truth was that others saw this behaviour as aggressive and commanding. *'What stings the most is that people are afraid of me,'* he went on. *'I never wanted to be that type of leader and person.'*

I get Saurabh to trust in his strengths

The moment called for acknowledgement of his strengths. He had taken a values-in-action strengths profile that ranks twenty-four professional strengths. This robust assessment of character strengths was developed[1] under the patronage of Marty Seligman, professor of psychology at the University of Pennsylvania, and Chris Peterson, late professor of psychology and organizational studies at the University of Michigan.

For Saurabh, curiosity had come out on top. He was a voracious reader and a knowledgeable, educated man. How might this strength extend to empathizing with other people's value systems? And how could he learn about their motivations in such a way that he could influence them rather than act aggressively or dismissively towards them, especially when it came to the more senior stakeholders, seeing as he had no formal authority over them?

There is an understandable scepticism in the world at large when it comes to assessing the extent to which one can quantify and measure human progress and growth. Human change is messy, it is complex, it takes time and there will be setbacks.

Metrics like those twenty-four professional strengths should never become a crutch on which the coach can lean their full weight. What we can do, however, is to cross-examine our data. In Saurabh's case, the feedback report also confirmed that many of his strengths were readily recognized by his raters: his smarts, his honesty, his courage, his results-oriented method of work, his humility and integrity, his curiosity about life in general as well as his interest in learning new skills.

Strengths are very important to define early on because they facilitate a leader's awareness of where they excel and where they may have blind spots. When applying their strengths, leaders feel deeply energized and quickly see learning curves that they can put into practice. They can apply their strengths in two ways: First, by finding the myriad ways in which to apply their 'high-performing' strengths (those that appear in the top ten of their strengths profile). A strength that we only use in one direction is a missed opportunity, so part of the work ahead was to clarify where Saurabh underused those strengths and how he could learn to play up his strengths in an effective and authentic way.

Second, a client can apply his strengths by toning them down. This is not usually a suggestion easily made to high-strung CEOs, but those top ten strengths can be detrimental to the leader and their team when they are overplayed. In Saurabh's case, his curiosity to find new business at every opportunity turned him into a taskmaster, both for himself and for those around him. And while his strong sense of integrity (another high-performing strength for him) offered him direction and created trust in him among others, this strength, when overused, also led him to believe that those who had different values from his own were misguided.

I understood the hurdle that we had to climb. As part of his appraisal by the executive search firm, he had taken the Hogan, a well-established psychometric assessment that offers insights into a leader's personality. As with most leaders, his profile showed that in tandem with whatever other changes we wanted to make, managing stress and setting boundaries were going to be key for any positive change to become visible. Taking care of himself was low on his list of priorities, well below work and providing for his family. Saurabh had too little time and too much stress—he was running on empty.

At my suggestion of focusing on his curiosity to help him reach his goals, Saurabh rose to the challenge. Our conversations went deeper, beyond the theory and tactics we had had to date. With my support, he identified the behaviours he needed to tweak, where to apply his strengths and how to measure progress.

We used a leadership development template to provide the structure for these actions and to define his goals. Here is an excerpt from Saurabh's first draft for one of his goals. It illustrates nicely how much work is invested in the coaching process.

Exhibit 3: Saurabh's Leadership Development Plan

Saurabh's Leadership Development Plan

1. What do I want to change?

Tip: Pick an area of focus that you are fully committed to bring forward (on a scale of 1-10, 10 being the most motivated, aim for a 7 or above).

Development focus	Timing (by when?)	Support required (by who?)
Manage my stress/emotions	*By February 2018*	*Coach, Direct Reports, Manager*

2. Why do I want this change?

What specific outcomes, both for myself and for others, do I envision as a result of this change?

1. *Be more relaxed, more engaged when I am with my family; give more time to the family, travel less and invest in life hygiene*

2. *Feel more connected to my professional peers and in general people I work with and for*

3. *Cultivate faith in the organization's corporate values, explore how my manager and I can see the world through similar lenses and build the foundations for a good Chairman and CEO relationship*

4. *Ensure others (including the Board) and I get to know each other better, both professionally and personally*

5. *Grow into an inspiring leader that motivates his teams and can successfully rally others to build a strong organization for the future*

Coaching is not only about supporting and challenging clients to meet their goals of change and growth. It is also about keeping a client's feet to the fire and holding them accountable on the way there. Accountability also means that we can assess and measure progress. To achieve this, Saurabh and I defined the metrics. These metrics included continuous feedback loops from stakeholders, his own sense of progress on a scale of 1 to 10, the number of open-ended questions he posed against the number of directives he gave, how much he delegated tasks and crucially, how frequently he lost his temper.

3. How: Implementing something every day

	What new behavior will I try?
	Where will I push myself out of my comfort zone? Who do I need to involve in this effort?
	What resources do I have available to reach my goal?
	How can I measure progress?

Context	Development Action	Support required	Review dates
Stress and emotion management	1. Delegate/time management: - Read 'Delegating with confidence' - Review my agenda: what to delegate, what to ditch, what to add that energizes; examples of ditching may be public speaking engagements that are not related to my role as future Group CEO;

2. Build self awareness: 10 min a day journal on one moment that energized me and one moment that stressed me & bring that journal to the coaching session; practicing my strength of perspective and judgement in novel ways

3. 2x Daily 5 min of Meditation and 4-5-6 breathing technique

4. Glass half full exercise: ask myself in every challenging situation: what is working, what else might be true | Coach; Direct Reports; | 15th Dec '17 |

Source: Dr. Ana Lueneburger, Fox meets Owl Limited

I made sure this plan went to that granular level I now knew Saurabh needed, and that it described the methods of progress in detail (what engaging with others might look like, who 'others' referred to, the timeframe, etc.). And remember that the leadership plan is a road map and that it is a working document that changes (sometimes significantly) over time as the client and/or the system (organization) evolves.

Three businessmen at a (gargantuan) oval table

For change to be effective, it has to be sustainable. And this means the environment in which the leader works must be supportive of such change. In an ideal scenario, the work environment will also shift in one dynamic wave towards positive change as a whole, along with the leader's change. The first chance for this to begin was during my meeting to discuss Saurabh's progress with the founder of the bank as the sponsor of the engagement, the lead partner at the executive search firm and Saurabh himself. Typically, I would also have invited an internal HR business partner, but the bank did not have a person in such a role at their in-house HR department at the time. The lead partner at the search firm would at least provide some neutral ground for us.

We know from research that even positive change can destabilize those involved. Wherever there is gain, there is also often a sense of loss: think of a move to a new position where excitement awaits but also the loss of familiar faces and networks. We also tend to experience loss up to four times greater than what we gain. Therefore, it isn't unusual to see acts of sabotage emerge in a leader's environment in resistance to the prospect of change. It is in our DNA to see change and uncertainty as threatening. This uncertainty awakens our instincts to fight change, even if it is going to be good for us. Bob Kegan, a long-time professor at Harvard and a researcher on human development, has done phenomenal research on this, defining resistance to change as having 'one foot on the brake and one foot on the gas',[2] leading to an impasse that prevents forward movement.

I joined the virtual meeting room from my office in London, and from that vantage point, I could watch how the three men entered the bank's boardroom in Mumbai. Despite our physical distance, the tension was palpable. The men chose to seat themselves at equal distances apart at the large oval table. I opened the meeting: *'Welcome to our first alignment meeting today where we have the opportunity to review the themes from the interview feedback and the goals that Saurabh based on the results. We are keen to have you as travel partners on this important journey and look forward to hearing your thoughts and suggestions as we look ahead.'* The bank's founder seemed to be carefully monitoring what he thought would unfold. Coaching had been an unknown quantity in the entrepreneurial structure that he had first launched in 1998 and, over the years, had successfully built into a fully-fledged investment bank. Not surprisingly, this setting was unfamiliar to him. Perhaps he was prepared for the same Saurabh.

I could only imagine his surprise when Saurabh spoke up, thanking them for their presence and eloquently describing the coaching experience to date. He then started to present the core patterns that had emerged from the 360-degree feedback interviews. As he shared some of the difficult feedback he had received openly and humbly, the energy in the room shifted. The other executives leaned in. They were engaged in what he had to say. The founder was very clearly taken by Saurabh's courage and vulnerability, sharing later that he felt it moved the needle between them, two men who had previously communicated mainly through an intermediary. He was hopeful that he and Saurabh might get to the point where they could have an open dialogue where they would accept some of their differences and put their combined energy into the investment bank. The idea that Saurabh might become the founder's successor was becoming more of a reality.

After the meeting, I wanted to hear from Saurabh. '*I feel more optimistic about the prospect of becoming the group CEO*,' he beamed. We were heading in the right direction.

When the safety net starts to strangle progress

For the second phase of the coaching process, commitment to goals and implementation of changes, Saurabh and I agreed to meet twice a month for ninety-minute sessions and assess his progress as we went along. Between sessions, Saurabh had free access to my time, schedules permitting. It seemed that the many articles I was sharing with him were read and absorbed in their entirety. This kind of vigour in a client infuses a real energy into the process and in me as a coach as well. It made me feel that his case stood a great chance of forward movement.

Nevertheless, the most challenging work for Saurabh was still to come. It is one thing to understand how to change new behaviours on a theoretical level and quite another to master them in practice. Theory had been a safety net for him, and yet that net had started to restrict his progress. How could he really shift from an autocratic leadership style to an inclusive 'leader as coach' style? How might he move from micromanaging behaviours to focusing on asking open-ended questions and encouraging direct reports to find their own path? And how could he make those direct reports embrace their newly won autonomy? Ultimately—how could he apply what he had learnt?

On an intellectual level, Saurabh had no trouble grasping the idea that efficiency was not the same as effectiveness.[3] Yet, I had my concerns about whether Saurabh, someone who could rarely stand still and who was described by his raters as 'a man in a hurry', would give himself the time to implement insights.

Another problem is that sabotaging behaviours rarely emerge on their own. In Saurabh's case, he seemed to firmly believe that resting or even slowing down would jeopardize the results he had achieved so far. And in his upbringing, he had learnt that pushing harder in the face of adversity bears fruit. These were deep-seated beliefs that were hard to change.

Taking Saurabh out of his comfort zone

Saurabh and I needed to speak about putting these concepts into practice. We would experiment a little, he would share his observations and then we would build on those responses. What gave me hope was that Saurabh's enthusiasm increased session by session, and while the work was hard, we also found moments of lightness. During these sessions, I admired Saurabh's ability to inject humour into his reflections and how unafraid he was to poke fun at himself. This lighter side showed up more frequently as the months went by. Setbacks on the way—an email sent in haste, a careless phrase to his colleagues—gave us opportunities to revisit these moments when he slipped and consider how he could have done better. Rather than manifesting as resistance, Saurabh's curiosity had begun to express itself as *resilience;* he faced adversity and used it to reflect on and learn more about himself.

With each session, I could see Saurabh grow exponentially. I could understand why the founder liked and cared for Saurabh, despite his temper. I imagined that having a young, talented rainmaker in the firm already warms the heart of any founder. An astute reader of people, the founder likely also enjoyed Saurabh's authenticity and honesty—something that he did not always get from those that wanted to be in the company of a hugely successful and influential man like himself. And yet I am still not sure if Saurabh ever fully trusted that the founder, who had a different business ethos, truly cared for him. He certainly always remained careful around him. Theirs was a complex relationship, and I had begun to wonder if there was a psychological underpinning to it all. And yet, while I am a fully trained and licensed therapist, coaching is not therapy. I had to make sure to not venture into areas beyond the scope of what a client signed up for. This, unfortunately, isn't always felt by every coach. Still, to the interested client reading this book, I give you fair warning: coaching currently doesn't strictly require professional training, and there are as many coaches as there are dentists. And boy, does going to the wrong dentist hurt!

Our coaching relationship blossoms in Mumbai

'*We are all really looking forward to you coming to Mumbai next week*,' Saurabh seemed enthusiastic. The date for my Mumbai visit was advancing. The purpose was for me to see Saurabh in his natural environment, meet with different stakeholders, including the board of the bank, and observe Saurabh in meetings. This last point can become a very powerful lever that offers invaluable insights into a leader's style of interacting with others.

Up to that point, Saurabh and I had only met in person once before. From the intensity of our conversations over those two months, it certainly didn't feel that way. I often observe *in situ* in my work with senior leaders, but I rarely travel as far as India. I stepped off the plane and into a humid wave in which I found it hard to breathe and was glad to get to the hotel that Saurabh had organized for my stay, with its air-conditioned foyer! When I got to the bank's headquarters the next morning, Saurabh came to welcome me with a warm smile. There is an authenticity to Saurabh that is palpable—this is an incredible strength which, when carefully deployed, keeps leaders in their element and helps their colleagues and peers to trust them.

He took me to the boardroom. Unlike many of its competitor banks, where every office and every corridor looks like the next, this bank's décor, its people and its location in the middle of a busy Mumbai neighbourhood carried a unique note to it. I truly appreciated this invitation to Saurabh's place of work and was also mindful that I had a big learning journey ahead for myself as well.

Cross-culture coaching: the elephant in the room

Here I was, a coach of German origin who has lived and worked in France, the US and the UK, partnering with a client of Indian origin with British education and training. Cultural differences can render coaching work more complex. Just visualize the cultures that were present in our two-person coaching partnership[4]:

Exhibit 4: Five cultures are in the coaching partnership

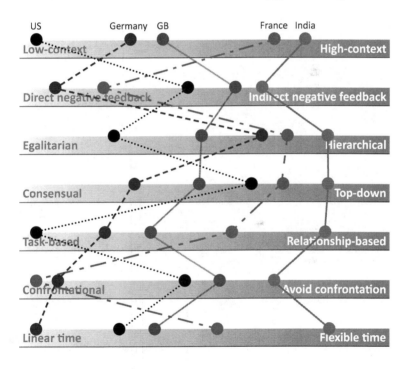

Source: Erin Meyer, The Country Mapping Tool

In many ways, cultural maps are meaning-making tools and allow us to understand how we tend to see the world and how others around us tend to see it. Yet, it is important to keep in mind that these are patterns or tendencies, not absolute truths. Individuals can exhibit values and behaviours that are quite different from their cultural reference group.

Exhibit 5: Ana's Culture Map

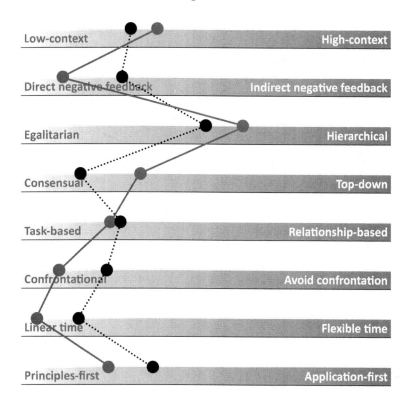

Source: Erin Meyer, The Country Mapping Tool

Exhibit 6: Saurabh's Culture Map

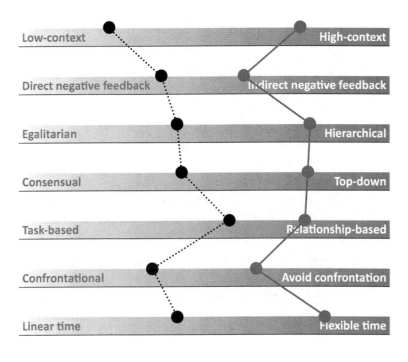

Source: Erin Meyer, The Country Mapping Tool

My map came out quite closely aligned with my country of origin, Germany. On the other hand, Saurabh's map resembled more closely that of a UK national than that of India, his country of origin. The main exception was his preference for prioritizing relationships over tasks. These individual maps also need to be seen as indicators, and it is important to confirm (or not) whether the visual result feels accurate.

Most critical is that coach and client are aware of cultural similarities and differences. In general, cultural patterns do influence how one communicates, how decisions are made, how trust is built. Not being aware of these tendencies risks negatively impacting performance. Saurabh's personal preference to engage in confrontation will struggle to land well in India. Yet, it may serve him well in more confrontational cultures such as France or Denmark.

As the coach, I am committed to remaining curious about cultural beliefs and behaviours in my client's context and minimizing cultural blind spots. I have worked in global environments with over fifty nationalities on site. I have also worked in cultures where I was the minority and had to find ways to understand and adapt to differences in the cultural weave. There are certainly also benefits to coaching across cultures. Different perspectives may emerge that trigger insight in a client. And heightened awareness is rarely where there is a comfort zone!

This visit to Mumbai felt priceless.

A small but important note on vulnerability

In the first of what would be many meetings with the founder, the board and the various stakeholders, I got yet another valuable insight into Saurabh's work, his leadership and how he interacted with others. Throughout the week, I became a 'fly on the wall' in Saurabh's meetings with his direct reports. Sitting in a corner of his room, I would observe his interactions with others. These were also opportunities to get a stronger understanding of his team. Saurabh and I debriefed after every one of these meetings to explore what emerged and how he might best leverage these findings.

One evening, towards the end of my visit, I went out for dinner with Saurabh and his wife, Sarbani. Even though I have to stress again that these projects are not therapy, as part of any work I do, I also try to grasp my clients' personal context. It is a very helpful way to get informed about their values, the consistency and balance of their work and home life, and simply who they are as people. Getting feedback from a client's trusted personal circle often reveals useful data that can help explain a leader's behaviour at work. I ask for permission to do this, and I respect whatever boundaries my client wants to set. Sarbani, who had also been involved in the 360-degree feedback interviews, came to offer valuable insights into Saurabh's past and his personal life.

I noticed that Saurabh and his wife were equals in their partnership, albeit with very distinct roles as parents to their two young children. I also sensed that Saurabh was devoted to his family and focused on creating a viable future for them. He took being the breadwinner seriously—a big responsibility, and one that added to the many pressures he already faced, internally and externally.

It was a lovely evening, but I remained mindful of the boundaries in place to protect the coach-client relationship. Aside from personal histories and experiences simply being a task for the therapist rather than the coach to unpick, vulnerability can beget vulnerability. This is an interesting field of tension that coaches frequently face: how firmly should you hold up that boundary between sharing and not sharing? As a trained psychotherapist, I would argue that boundaries are not very clinical in the world of coaching. However, the classic coach-training model on which many coaches orient themselves (as I did when I first started) states that we make it all about the client and hold our personal life and values back stringently. In its strictest interpretation, the coaching model asks that we remain Socratic partners to our clients—that we ask open-ended questions, that we seek permission to share our observations, and that we focus exclusively on the client's agenda and refrain from ever bringing our own stories into the dialogue. However, when you enter these fields, be they coaching or therapy, and when you accumulate experience, nuances will start to dissolve the edges of these boundaries. What works in theory also always needs to be understood—and sometimes adapted—when put into practice.

The art of coaching, then, is to strike a delicate balance between building a closer relationship and cultivating trust with bracketing anecdotes from the coach's world so that the client can fully own their coaching space.

A shock to the system

I left Mumbai in many ways with a new verve for life. The city had left its impression on me in so many ways, despite much of my time having been spent in office buildings! I saw that the city reflects in its people, who I still remember well for being so warm and generous with their time and help, whether it was during a visit to the Gandhi Museum or simply when asking for directions.

I also left Mumbai with the feeling that Saurabh and I had further cemented our trust in each other. I sensed that he deeply appreciated my visit and that I had travelled 4466 kilometres to see him in his environment and meet the key stakeholders. These were signs of my commitment to the business relationship and to his success.

The plane journey back to London gave me ample opportunity to reflect on this experience. I had given Saurabh feedback about his leadership from each observed meeting, and he would translate some of these learnings into behavioural action items. 'You need to ask more open-ended questions' was one piece of advice. The next day, Saurabh would begin his questions with 'How', 'What', 'When', and 'Tell me more'. The founder and he planned to foster a more active dialogue. I had already started to see how the team was feeling more empowered because of Saurabh's new leadership style. Saurabh himself seemed more centred and resilient in the face of continuing pressures at work. He had done a fantastic job in maintaining a healthy distance from the events that had once triggered him.

Saurabh and I were at the end of the fourth month of our six-month journey, and the third phase was about to begin. Phase three is about reaffirming goals, checking in with the client at the critical points you have defined together, measuring progress, adding specific behavioural tactics that will help the client to make the needed changes, celebrating wins and ensuring the client is accountable.

On our next Zoom call, though, Saurabh was in a state of shock: '*The bank is being challenged for advisory services rendered more than a decade and a half ago to a company that is now insolvent.*' He went on to explain that while these challenges were being made on dubious grounds and referred to a time before he had joined the bank, they contributed to the philosophical differences between himself and certain members of the bank's leadership team.

It does happen on occasion that an organization engages a coach for one of their business leaders and that, during that coaching, the leader concludes that his future does not lie with his employer. This can become a tricky situation for the coach. After all, the organization has hired and paid for her. But the coach is primarily there to support the leader and his or her professional goals. When Saurabh shared his thoughts with me about leaving the company, he could fully rely on my upholding confidentiality.

I suggested that he take some time to reflect on this decision. I knew from my coaching experiences that when under stress, some leaders might become more vulnerable to impulsive reactions. Was this one of those moments for Saurabh? Was he running away from something, or was he moving intentionally towards an inspiring future? To find out, I had to ask probing questions: Was this really the right decision for him? What might be speaking in favour of staying with the bank, and what could speak against it? If he were to fast-forward to his ninetieth birthday, what would really matter to him on looking back on his life? How might this reflection impact his decision now?

Saurabh was under a lot of pressure at work, so he was keen to evaluate what his next step was going to be. He had in the past shown his admiration for entrepreneurs—people who could take their curiosity to the very limits. '*Should I embark on realizing my dream of running my own business?*' he asked. After all, it would carry significant risks, such as losing the financial and structural security he had from holding a salaried position.

He was also concerned about the fate of the bank, should he leave it. He knew that they had no successor for his role. Despite the differences that alienated Saurabh from sections of the bank's leadership, he had developed a fondness for the founder that ran deep. Saurabh was loyal and remembered how the founder had put a lot of trust in him when he hired him eight years ago. Saurabh also admired the business empire that his employer had built from the ground up.

But Saurabh was also a man of principle. The bank's philosophy did not align with his own. And I could hear in his justifications exactly how tantalized he was by the prospect of being his own boss, building something himself and having more choice over when he could spend time with his wife and children.

The end of the story, the beginning of the franchise?

Closing out the coaching engagement typically requires the coach, the client and one or two key stakeholders to sit together and review the ground that has been covered. This discussion tends to focus on how many of the original goals were achieved and the key takeaways for the client and stakeholders. This is also the time to discuss any new goals that may have emerged and how a company might continue to support a leader's growth following the coaching engagement. In all, it's an integral part of the process.

Unfortunately, we couldn't set up this important closing-out session because the founder had to spend most of his time on his business commitments. I had attempted to reach him, but I was met with radio silence. It seemed there was nothing I could do. Instead, the closing out had to be done with each participant separately.

I called the partner at the executive search firm to share these developments and to thank him for his trust in me. Saurabh and I had an extensive conversation virtually, where I first heard that he was preparing to leave the bank. No more open-ended questions from me were necessary—he had already begun to share his intentions with internal colleagues. Keen not to leave any loose ends behind, he was busy preparing the business for his exit.

News of Saurabh's resignation was soon picked up outside the bank. India is a huge country. However, its business world, an intricate web of connections, is very small. Any news connected to business, therefore, spreads like wildfire, I learnt. It didn't take long for Saurabh to receive calls from people who wanted to join him in whatever new venture he was planning. Even though it was still rather vague at this stage as to what he would do after his resignation, the Saurabh brand was evidently strong, and many thought of it as likely to lead to future wealth and success if they associated with it.

These were all positive developments that had, in some way, been down to our coaching sessions. In the past, people had liked Saurabh despite his temper. They wanted to rally behind the autocrat. At this point, people liked Saurabh because of his drive to pull everyone towards a common goal.

Still, this ending was a bittersweet one for me. The engagement's core objective was to help Saurabh mature as a leader. But it also aimed to build a robust and direct rapport between the founder and Saurabh. That second objective was no longer possible, given the external developments and how much they highlighted the two men's conflicting business principles.

Within a week of Saurabh calling me to tell me that he had handed in his resignation, I received a note from the founder. He was visiting London again and wanted to meet up. This time we met in Home House on Portman Square, a private members' club. As I waited for the founder to arrive, I admired the club's dramatic fusion of décor, both old and new. How appropriate, considering that our meeting was also in an in-between space, after the coaching engagement and before the new beginnings for Saurabh away from the bank. It turned out that the founder wanted to find out from me if Saurabh's decision to move on was final. But this was not my call to make. I remember that the meeting was polite, friendly, and came as close as possible to that formal ending I craved, given that our engagement's protagonist was not present. I think we all mourned the end of this relationship in our own ways.

A great deal of growth . . . and some setbacks

I believe the coach-client relationship is a partnership of two that has the capability to impact multiple lives. I personally get huge satisfaction from helping others grow and become the best version of themselves. We are all 'works in progress' and using my experience and training to facilitate this growth is a unique privilege that I treasure. One of my clients, a CEO of a non-profit in downtown Manhattan, once summarized it beautifully: '*You coaches are multipliers; if you do good work with leaders, you touch not only them but also those whom they lead and influence.*'

Once Saurabh had resigned from the bank, we had fewer check-ins. Yet the foundations for a strong coach-client relationship had already been laid. He knew he could ping me any time, should he have a question or needed to share a thought. Given the intensity of coaching engagements, it can sometimes be difficult for clients to let go. Instead, they hold on to the relationship. It very rarely happens that contact ceases on the day of the close-out. Contact ebbs and flows over time, and both parties are aware of each other's presence even during long periods of silence.

A few months on, Saurabh reached out to tell me that he was going to pass through London in the summer as part of a business trip. He invited me to lunch, so I picked one of my favourite sushi houses in London, the Michelin-starred Sake no Hana (sadly, it's no longer around), close to St James. Saurabh smiled as he announced that he would soon launch his own business. It didn't surprise me that he was about to start his own asset management firm. He had reached this decision after much soul-searching. Over our plates of neatly arranged sashimi and maki, he told me that he had been thinking of this during our work together. The crystallization of ideological differences within the bank was what sealed the deal. After consulting a few trusted friends, he had taken the plunge. My theory of positive impact was put into practice so very soon.

In my fourteen years of working with senior leaders, there always comes a moment when I have to give advice. It's not easy to do—coaches are trained not to dish out suggestions but rather help them identify the path they always knew inside themselves they wanted to take. In fact, at the start of my career as a coach, I worked with a senior client who was quite lost and unsure about his role, yet I kept upholding the Socratic model. I refused to believe I should do anything more than listen and reflect. It took my supervisor Dr Carol Kauffman, founder of the Institute of Coaching at Harvard Medical School, to finally say: '*Oh, Ana, just go ahead and tell him what to do!*' She had seen what my as-yet-untrained eyes could not see: that even though we learn the theory that we must only act as reflections for our clients, in practice, the occasion can sometimes call for us to be hands-on and advise clients on what to do. In the years that have passed, I have become more confident in understanding when to do this. Senior leaders deserve to benefit from the decades of experience coaches have and hear our thoughts. The key is to see when they need it, make sure that we get their permission before giving them advice, and that they are aware that they are always in control of their own path, whatever decision they do make.

Of course, not every client will need or want this. They may prefer more nuance from a coach. Or they might initially resist it. As I had already been working with Saurabh for many months, I knew he was fiercely independent and unlikely to be swayed by my opinion alone. I felt that even though my advice was at this point necessary, I would have some work to do in bringing him around to receiving it in the proper spirit.

But I could see why Saurabh had asked me to lunch. This was not just a friendly check-in. Saurabh acknowledged that launching a new business would be hard and that raising the funds he needed to sustain the business would take a while.

I was convinced: if anyone could do it, it would be Saurabh. But he needed reassurance: *'You have a strong track record of persevering against the odds, both personally and professionally. Your excitement about this venture is palpable. And a leader with passion is far more likely to succeed.'*

We explored how he and I might work together as he entered this new chapter, and in the two years that followed, we had periodic but no less intense contact. He founded Marcellus, and we discussed my coming on as a member of the board. It was all going to plan. Marcellus was just starting to see growth. And then, the global pandemic hit.

Emerging businesses like Saurabh's were hit hard, especially those in the early stages of growth. He called me to ask what he could do and how he might support his team during this crisis. He was no longer the leader who would drive his team hard, whatever the circumstances. He was a leader who deeply cared about the people who worked for and with him.

Other people matter

Saurabh's ability to withstand pressure had increased manifold as part of our work together. Of course, he had always managed to cope, but the harmful by-product of Saurabh's stress was anger and frustration with his team. The challenges he now faced as a new business owner only increased, especially as the pandemic took its toll. Marcellus was growing despite the global pandemic, and team members were starting to show signs of burnout as their mental and physical resources were depleted. And yet, through it all, Saurabh's new-found resilience helped support himself and his team, even in times of extreme stress.

A final significant visible change was that Saurabh embraced the idea that he was no longer the lone man fighting the battles. He had come to trust that his colleagues were by his side and that he could count on them. He no longer considered differences in opinion to be an unsolvable problem. Most fundamentally, Saurabh now sought connection with others. One of my mentors, the late Chris Peterson, founding father of the strength movement in the US and professor of positive psychology at the University of Michigan, once told me so poignantly: *'Other people matter.'*

I wonder if it is the safe space of coaching, where we personally relate to our clients and, in that way, model a nurturing relationship, that allows healing to begin. When coach and client trust each other, the client can enter a safe space to explore their (hi)story and how it has shaped them. It is also a space where clients can gain a deeper understanding of themselves, their values, their triggers and what leads to their professional behaviours, positive or negative. And while tangible change is often desirable, it is even more important that clients have a choice as to how they show up. They become free agents and decision-makers, having shed the attitude of simply being on autopilot in their careers.

This is the most rewarding part of the work coaches are privileged to do—helping others unlock their full potential. It is here where we experience that we also matter, as we can offer impact well beyond the boundaries of our coaching relationship. And this is where I personally find that sense of purpose that so many of us crave in our short time on this earth.

Key Takeaways

- Coaching is a high-impact experience that requires clients to venture into unknown and often uncomfortable (but ultimately, often very rewarding) territory.
- A typical coaching engagement runs between six and twelve months. It involves three phases: 1) Discovery and Trust

Building, 2) Commitment to Goals and Implementation, and 3) Reinforcement of Change and looking ahead post the coaching engagement.

- Trust between coach and client is the backbone for any change. There are sometimes surprisingly small elements that can cement trust.
- Feedback from stakeholders offers insight into a client's agenda for change and is often the key milestone to accelerate forward movement.
- Coach and client must be flexible and remember that the leadership plan with its goals is a road map and that it is a working document that changes (sometimes significantly) over time as the client and the system (organization, key stakeholders, circumstances) evolve.

If you realize your wildest dreams can hurt you

And your appetite for pain has drunk its fill

I ask of you a very simple question

Did you think for one minute that you are alone?

From 'Just Wait' (1994), Blues Traveler

CHAPTER 3

In a Nutshell: The Client's Perspective
Saurabh's reflections

The toughest chapter to write

I have been writing books for more than a quarter of a century. In fact, I wrote my first book to pay my way through university. Since then, I have authored or co-authored five bestsellers, not to mention hundreds of columns for newspapers and websites. However, the words that follow in this chapter are by far the hardest bit of writing I have ever done.

Economics, finance, corporate strategy—in general, anything related to other people's lives—are relatively straightforward subjects for me to write on because I am using facts and my formal training to analyse information and share my perspectives with the reader. By profession, I am trained to analyse other people and their businesses. Writing about myself is an altogether different challenge because, by definition, I cannot be 'objective' about myself. Hence I find it deeply discomfiting when, rather than my showing the mirror to others, the situation is reversed and I have to face the mirror. In fact, I find the very idea of anything written about me so entirely off-putting that I have repeatedly turned down requests from notable authors who have offered to write my biography. In one of these cases, I even went so far as to read published books by the biographer (which were very impressive) but I simply could not muster enough faith in myself and in her to go ahead with the project.

Writing about oneself is even harder when the subject at hand is a cathartic experience. As I wrote the words that follow, I kept fretting and worrying about a range of questions from 'Am I being too honest about myself?' to 'Does anyone really want to know how I have developed as a person or how my coach helped me?' In the end, as part of my journey with Ana, to understand myself and to become a better version of myself, we felt that writing this chapter and this book would indeed be a step forward. Furthermore, as Ana has explained in the opening chapter of this book, not only could our story help us understand our own journeys (as a leader and a coach, respectively), it might also help others who find themselves at a similar juncture in their careers. So, here is my journey of change—presented in black and white to the world at large.

My request to the board

I have many weaknesses, but they haven't stopped me from being a serial high achiever. I was a prize-winning student at high school in England. At university, I was an ace economics student at the London School of Economics (LSE), and to pay my way through LSE, I authored a book on finance, which remains in print to this day with a cover price of over US$100.[1] By the time I turned thirty, I had co-founded a profitable start-up in London and was rated as one of the top small-cap equity analysts in the UK. Bolstered by this track record, by the time I turned forty, I had steered a leading broking and investment management franchise in Mumbai from the red to the black and had been rated as India's leading equity strategist for three years in a row. But was that enough? No way—chasing new worlds to conquer was a way of life for me. For as long as I can remember, I have pushed myself as hard as I can, tried to learn as much as I can, tried to take on ever-more-challenging assignments and rise in the world.

So, it was in keeping with my character that in December 2016, at a specially convened meeting on the first floor of the Oberoi Hotel on Marine Drive, Mumbai, I told the board of directors of my erstwhile employer that I wanted to be the group CEO rather than just the CEO of the investment management and broking business.

The board wasn't convinced. They said I needed to be tested and assessed to see if I was fit for the role. One of the world's leading executive search firms was hired to interview me, test me and assess me. Their verdict, after subjecting me to a battery of tests and many hours of interviews, was that while I was a bright, hardworking individual with a credible track record of leadership, I had some way to go before I could be given greater responsibilities. My shortcomings—as per this report—were a tendency to fly off the handle when dealing with people I didn't like, a low emotional quotient (EQ) and a 'moody and irritable' nature. In addition, I was also 'naturally suspicious' of people. Even though more than six years have passed since I first read the headhunter's diagnosis of me, I can recite from memory most of their ten pages of analysis of my strengths and weaknesses.

Once the verdict from the experts was in, the recommendation from my bosses was that I get a coach to help me rectify the gaps in my skillset. As one would expect, I was not happy about the situation. I felt that if you interviewed and tested someone for hours on end and asked dozens of smart people around that person for feedback, you were bound to find shortcomings. To then ask that person to be subjected to coaching to rectify these deficiencies appeared to me—at that stage in my life and in the frame of mind I was in then—to be the work of corporate politics. In the interest of furthering my career, I sensed I did not have much choice but to accept the recommendation.

The executive search firm was then asked to propose two qualified coaches for me. The first was an American lady who was now working out of Europe, and the second was Ana, a German national who had worked in New York for over a decade and was now working globally, based out of London. I spoke to both coaches in separate videoconference calls. In those pre-Zoom days, the videoconference screen took up one end of the boardroom of my employer's office. So, when I spoke to Ana for the first time in the spring of 2017, her smile and the confidence she radiated quite literally lit up the room!

I knew I had to play along with the board's desire to see me get coached. Therefore, I was looking for a coach who would not impose a lot of demanding assignments in what was already a long working day for me. In other words, I was looking for a coach who would let me do the talking and then not give me that much to do. I chose Ana because she seemed to fit the bill. Within six months, I realized that I had misread Ana's friendliness as being indicative of someone who was willing to accommodate my desire for an undemanding coach. Thankfully, my misreading of Ana's personality was one of the best mistakes I made in my professional career!

Looking back at those months in early 2017, I realize now how badly I needed a coach then. By that stage of my career, I was an angry and irritable middle-aged executive. I had spent much of the previous decade on what felt like an endless treadmill of chasing annual budgets (which kept getting bigger every year), long-haul flights (which kept becoming more frequent every year, leaving me permanently jet-lagged), the quest for bigger bonuses and the downside of all this: lower back problems, headaches, sleeplessness and, increasingly, less time spent with family and with the people closest to me. In retrospect, becoming group CEO wasn't going to solve anything for me. In fact, my wife, Sarbani, had pointed out to me that exhaustion and the relentlessness of what I was doing had made me become more impatient and less considerate as an individual. But, looking back at the time period of 2010–17, I was not in the mood to listen to anyone.

The coach enters the picture

I met Ana for the first time in person at a coffee shop on Coleman Street in the financial district of London in summer 2017. I can distinctly remember being bone-tired after three days of non-stop meetings with clients in London. I was looking forward to boarding the flight to New York, having a glass of wine with a nice meal and going off to sleep. While I had misgivings about the coaching exercise, I didn't voice them fully in my kick-off meeting with Ana because of the imperative from the board that I get coached. Ana asked to me explain what I wanted to get out of the coaching exercise. I did so in writing. Here is an excerpt of what I wrote in the intake form that Ana asked me to fill out:

Question: What complaints do you think your direct reports have about you? How do you think they would like you to change?

Answer (mine): *I am short-tempered and sometimes can be very volatile. I would like to lose my temper less and become a calmer leader.*

I work very hard myself and expect others to do the same. Unfortunately, this sort of sustained intensity breaks other people—physically and psychologically—and they often just give up because they can't keep up with me. I want to learn how to make people deliver outstanding performance without breaking them.

I am sceptical of mainstream business thinking, sceptical of the rubbish that gets taught in most business schools and sceptical of the nonsense that gets published in glossy business magazines. Unfortunately, most people who come to work in investment banking come from these business schools and read these useless business magazines. I give them a very hard time and over three to five years, force them to rewire their thinking about life and business.

Given the values that my parents have instilled in me, I don't set a great deal of store by money. I don't come to work thinking how much money I will make and I expect my team members to also take a dispassionate view of money. Most investment bankers find this very hard—their life revolves around money and material possessions and often they leave us for other places which they believe will make them richer quicker.

Ana and I began our fortnightly coaching sessions in September 2017. The sessions were two hours long and exhausting. There was pre-reading to be done and exercises to be completed. It was hard work. However, even as I doubted the usefulness of the exercise, I found the reading material interesting. From the fortnightly coaching sessions that took place in the summer and monsoon of 2017, I remember two of these pieces with particular fondness.

The first was an *HBR* article, 'The Power of Small Wins'.[2] Given that, directly and indirectly, I managed a team of around 100 people, I had for good reason been interested in helping my team increase its productivity. My style of boosting productivity was to set transparent stretch targets and then use the carrot-and-stick approach to push the team to meet these targets. By 2017, I realized that while my style of managing people worked, it had its limitations, especially when it came to the more mature team members, i.e., people in their late thirties and forties. This article showed me that there was a different way to achieve the same. It said:

> What motivates people on a day-to-day basis is the sense that they are making progress. Managers who take this finding to heart will easily see the corollary: The best thing they can do for their people is provide the catalysts and nourishers that allow projects to move forward while removing the obstacles and toxins that result in setbacks.

After reading this piece, I remember asking every team I managed to organize celebratory drinks every month, a practice that my current colleagues have more skilfully implemented than I was ever able to.

The second piece was from the *Guardian* and it was about the power of language—more specifically about the power of specific words—to sway people to do what you want them to do.[3] The article said that '*certain words and phrases have the power to change the course of a conversation*'. The article, based on research conducted by Elizabeth Stokoe, professor of social interaction at Loughborough University, used plenty of examples to explain '*It's not what you say, it's how you say it*':

> Stokoe found that people who had responded negatively when asked if they would like to attend mediation seemed

to change their minds when the mediator used the phrase, 'Would you be willing to come for a meeting?' . . . As soon as the word 'willing' was uttered, people would say: 'Oh, yes definitely'—they would actually interrupt the sentence to agree.

I studied this article carefully and began inserting certain keywords into my interactions with others.

In fact, thanks to the reading material Ana shared with me, I got drawn into the wealth of research conducted by psychologists on productivity and creativity and what drives these types of qualities, both at the level of the individual and at the level of the team. Three years later, my research and reading in this area would result in my co-writing a bestselling book on this subject—*The Victory Project: Six Steps to Peak Potential*[4]— with my friend Anupam Gupta.

Moving back to 2017, as I read and reflected and spoke to Ana, over the course of the next six months I started shedding my insecurities and feeling progressively more relaxed about my abilities. She made me focus on my strengths. She helped me beat up myself less about my weaknesses. Slowly, the mental fog started abating. Slowly, I started pushing my mind and my body less. Then I started pushing my colleagues and team less.

The heart of the coaching engagement

Ana and I started building clarity on my strengths and weaknesses—something that I had never really thought about much until that point. Ana visited Mumbai in the autumn of 2017 and talked to my colleagues and my bosses to build further clarity on the subject. To protect the confidentiality of my raters and encourage them to be open, she didn't tell me what they told her, but her Socratic style of questioning helped me understand my strengths and weaknesses, my likes and dislikes, and how I came across to those around me. Broadly speaking, by the time Diwali firecrackers were being burst in November 2017, I had realized that:

- I was good at working hard to think through tricky issues in finance, economics and business, and communicating those to clients. Alongside that, over the years, I had also learnt how to hire and motivate smart people.
- However, I struggled with knowing how to effectively push myself and my colleagues to work very hard over extended periods of time. I would often go beyond my own physical limits and would end up criticizing senior colleagues in front of others (inside the firm) and public leaders on broadcast and print media (outside the firm). As a result, I was quite firm if not rigid in my views and often failed to form deep relationships with colleagues and clients. I knew that a skilled adviser needs to build these connections with clients to anticipate and understand their needs, often even before the clients themselves are aware of them. However, I found it hard to act on this insight into client behaviour.

While, with the benefit of several years of hindsight, I am able to summarize the feedback that Ana gave me in the fall of 2017 into the neat bullet points listed above, truth be told, in real time (i.e., back in October 2017) the feedback that Ana gave me hurt—the criticism stung in a way that no feedback that I had received in my corporate career had. In fact, even with the benefit of many years of distance between 2017 and the current day, when I re-read the feedback that Ana gave me back then, it still feels as if someone is sprinkling red chilli powder on my soul. I reckon that's because what Ana did—very cleverly and to great effect—was to spend a lot of time speaking in person to people whom I worked closely with, and then put down on paper, without any sugar-coating (at least, that's what it felt like), what these people had told her about me.

The people whom I worked with closely were some of India's most respected corporate professionals—they were either my bosses or board members of my then employer. Most of them were at least fifteen years older than me and highly accomplished—in fact, celebrated—professionals in their own right. What Ana's feedback told me in blunt language was that not only did I not spend enough time with them (something they had asked me to several times in the years gone by), but also that when I did talk to them it was in a highly transactional context, when I needed them to do something for me.

My feedback report also told me that if I did not get what I wanted (or what I needed from them), I would explode in front of them and behave like a brat. I could go on and on, but I hope I have given you a clear enough picture of my 'Dr Jekyll and Mr Hyde'[5] persona at that point: When it came to the intellectual side of getting the job done and bringing in the revenues, I was Dr Jekyll; the Mr Hyde aspect came into play when it came to more complex matters hinging on delicate corporate relationships and matters of tact, understanding and emotional intelligence. For example, suppose a fifty-something colleague who has worked hard for thirty years is up for promotion to the role of 'managing director' for the fifth time in a decade, should I sign off the promotion (because if I don't, the colleague will quit) or should I hold back the promotion (because while the man works very hard, he's not a leader)? What I hadn't realized at that time is there are no easy answers to such questions. What I presumed at that point in time—incorrectly, as it turned out—is that the commercial success of the business that I had been tasked with managing gave me the licence to get away without investing emotionally in a bunch of relationships with people older and wiser than me.

Courtesy of the coaching, I had started figuring out of my own accord some of the points I have highlighted in the preceding paragraph. The written feedback report from Ana brought home to me all of my shortcomings very effectively, and that got the analytical part of my brain—the Dr Jekyll part—fully engaged in how to move forward and sort things out. Having been through a difficult upbringing during my teenage years as my parents grappled with financial and emotional challenges, I had learnt early on in life that when you suffer setbacks, you are faced with a choice between (a) moping and cursing your luck; or (b) applying yourself and your brain to chalk out a plan of action that will take you to a better place. And once you frame difficult situations in this language, provided you can muster the strength, you will go with option (b). The first step for me was to figure out why I was behaving the way I was, and this is where Ana's coaching really started clicking into high gear.

As Ana started helping me build a picture of what I was and wasn't strong in, I began realizing that this desire to be the group CEO of the company I was working with was a waste of time and effort on my part—it would neither allow me to play to my strengths nor do the things I enjoy the most. Instead, using the pretext of seeking promotion, I would end up trying to persuade myself to not only become a very different person but I would also potentially end up trying to become just the kind of corporate drone that I had no affection or affinity for.

During Ana's trip to Mumbai, other than collecting and giving me candid feedback, Ana organized something else which, with the benefit of hindsight, proved to be very helpful. One evening, my wife Sarbani and I went out to dinner with Ana and her husband Christoph. We went to a nice restaurant in Bandra, and over a bottle of wine and a hearty Rajasthani dinner, we couples got to know each other a bit better. Christoph and Ana told us about their lives, how they had met at INSEAD in Fontainebleau, got married, and were leading engaging but demanding corporate lives, first in Europe, then in the US and now in the UK. Between their roles in headhunting firms, in private equity and in coaching, they had raised their daughter. As Sarbani and I drove home that night, I felt that I had glimpsed the future. I felt that I had a picture—albeit a vague picture at that point in time—of what life could be like if I slowed down a bit and invested in relationships with the people whom I loved, the people whom I cared for, the people whose happiness mattered to me and the people whom I wanted to be loved by. I also saw that Sarbani—whose emotional intelligence is several notches higher than mine—had enjoyed the evening too. That convinced me that this vision of myself and my life going forward was worth introspecting on further. It was time to not just look at the man in the mirror; it was time to sort out the man in the mirror.

Years later, as I look back at what transpired in 2017, I realize that the dinner that Sarbani and I had with Ana and Christoph was a pivotal point in my relationship with Ana. At one level, nothing of any great importance was discussed that evening. In fact, we did not discuss business at all over that dinner.

What that dinner did allow me was to trust Ana more and see the extent to which she was willing to go to help me achieve my goals. I am a naturally suspicious person, this in part being rooted in my experiences of the past, which we will discuss in the subsequent chapters of this book. By making the effort to fly to India, by spending time with my colleagues in my office, by taking the time out to get to know my wife and by allowing us to get to know her husband, Ana was helping me understand that she was there to support me. It reinforced my feeling that her feedback to me was not driven by a Machiavellian corporate imperative. In real time, while these efforts were being made, I could not consciously grasp the importance of these trust-building initiatives, but in retrospect, I realize that in their absence there was a real risk that I would have ignored Ana's feedback and just got on with 'business as usual'.

Reflecting on feedback and trying to change

In the autumn of 2017, my family and I travelled for a short break to the holy city of Amritsar, home to the holiest shrine of the Sikhs, the Golden Temple. We checked into our hotel at around 2 p.m., and by the time we reached the temple, dusk was descending on Amritsar. I remember sitting next to the large water tank that surrounds the Golden Temple shrine and soaking up the atmosphere and the history of the temple. I remember seeing inscribed on the wall of the Golden Temple the names of generations of Indians who had laid down their lives for a cause they believed in. I remember looking at Sarbani and my two children, Jeet and Malini, and realizing that a life well lived is a life lived pursuing a cause that you believe in. Broking, block deals and fund-raises for large companies were clearly not that cause, I felt, as I took a picture of my family, which remains my phone screensaver to this day—a permanent reminder of the impact of the Golden Temple epiphany on my life. As we left the Golden Temple and drove towards the India–Pakistan border checkpoint at Wagah, I remember clearly understanding at that point that I was at a crossroads, and that one path would have me spend the next decade doing transactional financial deals and feeling unhappy about the soullessness of it all.

So, what was the cause that I believed in? And what was it that I enjoyed? I went back to Ana with those questions, and

Ana helped me confront them through the closing months of 2017. As part of this process of introspection on purpose and meaning, I (briefly) thought about quitting my job to become a full-time writer, as my first two books had both become bestsellers. But on further reflection, I realized that writing was a little too introverted a vocation for a person like me, who enjoys the buzz of working with other bright, hard-working people.

As we entered the closing months of 2017, I reflected deeply on who I really was versus what people perceived me to be versus who I wanted to become. In parallel to working with Ana, I read voraciously about the psychological origins of identity and desire. Two books on this subject influenced me deeply.

The first was *The Wisdom of Finance: Discovering Humanity in the World of Risk and Return* by Mihir Desai, an economist who teaches finance at Harvard Business School.[6] In his book, Desai presents the conventional principal-agent problem in economics in a novel way. Rather than just explaining the standard paradigms of, say, how the CEO of a company is the agent while the shareholders are the principal, Desai proposes that such principal-agent problems can be found in everyday life, and especially so in situations that we do *not* conventionally associate with principal-agent problems. For example, because of the influence that parents have on their children's psyche, parents are their children's principals (and the children, by that definition, their agents) long after the children have grown up and left the parental home. This implies that as a forty-year-old CEO in Mumbai, I might fancy myself to be my 'own man', but in reality, I could still be playing out the role that my parents wanted me to.

The second book that struck a chord in those months of deep introspection was a 1978 work by French philosopher and professor of literature at Stanford University, Rene Girard. In the book, *Things Hidden Since the Foundation of the World*,[7] Girard's remarkably original and—to my mind—powerful hypothesis of 'mimesis' unfolds sequentially:

1. Human beings have an innate desire to compete with each other and rise in the world. At the outset, this desire to compete and create new things and conquer new frontiers is a healthy thing as it spurs creativity, innovation and differentiation.

2. Then a complication kicks in, because human beings are social animals. They learn from each other and they copy each other. As a result, we start coveting the same things others do. For example, in isolation, I have no incentive to covet a diamond, which to my mind is a worthless stone. However, if twenty people around me begin coveting diamonds (or admission for their children into a certain school or flats on Altamount Road in Mumbai or holiday villas in Tuscany), then I too am likely to covet the same. Girard calls this mimicking of each other's desires 'mimesis'.

3. As hordes of people start seeking the same things, competition (or 'mimesis', as Girard calls it) intensifies. Then, in the heat of the battle, differentiation takes a back seat as all of us strive to outdo each other in acquiring these symbols of prestige. The logical escalation of this competitive battle is aggression vis-à-vis each other, which sometimes culminates in violence.

4. During this period of intense competition, as unhappiness increases and grievances multiply, society seeks a scapegoat. The scapegoat is deemed to be responsible for all of society's grievances, although, in reality, the grievances arise from mimesis.

As I soaked up Ana's coaching, I realized that my upbringing and my past had left mental scars that I needed to deal with. Like many other Indian professionals, I grew up in a family of modest means. My father was a structural engineer in a government-owned company and my mother was a maths teacher. My parents migrated from Kolkata to Delhi when I was a year old, and some of the most abiding memories of my childhood are my parents' protracted discussions on how they were struggling to make ends meet. In 1991, we—as a family—migrated to the UK. My parents were in their mid-forties by the time we migrated, and my sister and I were eleven and fifteen years old, respectively. What followed were five tough years in which all four of us were pushed to our limits—emotionally, physically and financially. More than three decades later, I can still see the impact of those tough years of the early 1990s on my parents, my sister and myself. For example, to this day, both my sister and I deal with challenges by going into our minds, introspecting and thinking things through. As Ana describes in the closing chapters of this book, this ability of mine—to live inside my mind—is a strength which, when overused, becomes a weakness.

I remember that I started working in 1992 when I was sixteen. For the remainder of my school and college years in London, I worked and studied pretty much non-stop, partly because I had no other choice and partly because I was determined to haul myself and the family to a better financial position. Those difficult years in the early 1990s, when we had next to nothing and when challenges used to hit the family one after another, left in me a deep desire to succeed. To give credit to the British education system and job market, I discovered that if I pushed myself hard enough, I could keep achieving more.

These early traumas and successes impacted me in other ways too. I inadvertently grew up very fast and took responsibility for managing 'grown-up' things early on in life. For example, I remember admitting my father to hospital late one night in 1993 when he fell seriously ill after a trip to India. I walked home from the hospital at 2 a.m. (we didn't own a car and there was no public transport late at night), slept for five hours and woke up at 7 a.m. so that I could reach work by 8 a.m. At lunchtime, I went to school for four hours before going back to work. After work, I went to see how my father was doing in the hospital. Then I returned home, made myself a dinner of soup and boiled vegetables and fell asleep listening to BBC World Services' nine o'clock news on my clapped-out Panasonic transistor radio, which I had retrieved from a roadside rubbish dump. At that time I thought all of this was normal for a teenager. It is only when I went to university that I realized that most teenagers live a very different sort of life, partying and going to concerts and restaurants. The typical bill for an evening of partying that my friends in university were accustomed to was what I earned in a whole week!

My upbringing, however, taught me a different sort of lesson—that you have to be strong so that you can lend strength and support to your relatives, friends and colleagues. To this day, when I see selfish leaders, I struggle to empathize with them—a problem which we will discuss in more detail in the penultimate chapter of this book.

In such circumstances, I started looking around for role models. When I entered the financial markets in London in my early twenties, I encountered outspoken, aggressive, brash and financially successful people. Even though my personality was neither outspoken nor brash, I began subconsciously modelling myself on these people, much as Girard's mimetic theory had predicted. And, as I rose through the ranks of my erstwhile employer's organization, I lost sight of my underlying personality and became a caricature of the pushy, uppity people

I had seen so often in the world of broking and trading. Ana's coaching sessions and her candid feedback made me realize that I needed to snap out of my mimetic desires and find and embrace my own underlying identity. I needed to become a person I was happy being rather than a twenty-first-century Indian version of Gordon Gekko.[8]

During Christmas 2017, I travelled to the Andaman and Nicobar Islands archipelago in the Bay of Bengal for our New Year's break with the extended family. On my long walks on the pristine beaches of Havelock Island, it dawned on me that asset management can answer both the questions that had occupied my mind of late (raised in the preceding paragraphs of this chapter)—namely, what is the cause I believe in and what is it that I enjoy. But I was unsure as to whether I had the means—financial and psychological—to build a successful asset management business in a market like India, where almost all the leading asset management firms are subsidiaries of giant financial services conglomerates. On the last day of that Andaman holiday—in the first week of 2018—I sat on the balcony of our hotel in Port Blair reading *No More Worlds to Conquer* by Chris Wright.[9] The book took its name from the story of Alexander the Great, the mighty conqueror from Macedon in the fourth century BCE, weeping as he lay dying. And why was Alexander weeping? He was weeping because he had no more worlds to conquer.

For his book, Wright had travelled the globe, tracking down an assortment of high achievers. From the astronaut who turned to painting to the World Cup-winning footballer who became an undertaker, each had grappled with the challenge of finding meaning once their fame had faded. I found the psychological journeys of the American astronauts in the book the most moving. For a fighter pilot anywhere in the world, the peak of her profession is to go to the moon.

What do you do with your life *after* you have walked on the surface of the moon? How do you quite literally come back down to earth and find meaning and purpose in your life? I realized that part of my mental struggle was not dissimilar— at that point, for each of the preceding three years, I had been ranked as India's leading equity strategist. From an intellectual perspective, my job had lost its appeal, and I realized that a significant part of my desire to become group CEO was an attempt to inject meaning and purpose into my career. I also realized that some of my counterproductive emotional outbursts were a manifestation of this frustration—that intellectually the job I was doing was now a dead end, and therefore I was operating at full throttle but with no purpose and with little sense of direction.

As I sat reading that book in the first week of 2018, I realized that to inject fresh meaning and purpose into their lives, the legends profiled in Chris Wright's book had deliberately moved on to something completely new, something that offered them a different challenge, something that was difficult but within the realms of achievability. One of the astronauts became a painter of lunar landscapes; another become a singer. Those who could not find new challenges, or new worlds to conquer, tended to see their minds, their lives and their relationships dissolve into nothingness. Around tea time, Sarbani told me that we needed to get into the taxi to the airport to get back home. By the time our flight landed in Mumbai four hours later, I knew that the time had come to move on from my quest to 'conquer the world'.

The deeper realization in January 2018 was that I have nothing to prove to anyone, no need to conquer any more worlds. I was and am the master of my destiny. As William Ernest Henley wrote in his stirring poem, *Invictus*:

It matters not how strait the gate,
How charged with punishments the scroll,
I am the master of my fate,
I am the captain of my soul.[10]

A month later, I quit my job.

Quitting my job and launching Marcellus

Over the next five months, I explained to my colleagues why I was leaving. Then I handed over my responsibilities to my direct reports, said my goodbyes to the clients and colleagues who had helped build what was by then (and remains to this day) a muscular financial services franchise in India and went home to put my feet up. My message to my clients and colleagues was that the franchise was in great shape and would continue to prosper. It was a message I sincerely believed in, and more than six years on I am delighted that the franchise continues to thrive and win accolades. I remember for the first seventy-two hours in June 2018 after I had stopped working, I felt every muscle, every sinew in my body relax—in a way they hadn't the past eight years.

All of that being said, I had resigned from my job without a clear picture of what I would do after quitting. I had served out my notice period in the first half of 2018 with a mixture of apprehension (about what the future held for my family and for me) and excitement (about the whole wide world of opportunities that beckoned).

I called Ana in the summer of 2018 to tell her that I was now a free agent and was trying to see if I could launch an asset management company. She offered to help me deal with the trials and tribulations that both of us presumed would inevitably follow. We met in St James' in London in the first week of July 2018. Anna treated me to a fabulous meal at a Japanese restaurant next to the building where once upon a time journalists of *The Economist* newspaper used to work.

I met my parents and my wider family that same week in London and explained to them why I had quit my job. Many of my relatives were shocked at my decision to quit a well-paid job, given that I had a young family to support. Undeterred, my wife Sarbani and I flew to Spain for a holiday. Neither of us knew what our next source of income would be, and there we were, a middle-aged couple with two young children to raise in a country like India, which has no social security safety net. As we did the maths on our savings using the calculator on my wife's phone, it wasn't quite clear to us that we had enough money to even finance our children's university education. Were we insane?

Sarbani and I have known each other since we were four years old and she moved into the New Delhi apartment block where I lived with my family. For a while, we even went to the same school, until my lack of interest in studies prompted my parents to move me to a more activity-oriented school in a different part of town. When Sarbani was sixteen and I seventeen, I mustered up all the courage I had in my testosterone-soaked teenage brain and asked her out for a date. Seven turbulent years later, we were married, and another decade and a half later we were the parents of two children about to enter their teens. In short, we had been through a lot together and knew that we would figure out a way forward in life—a well-paid full-time job was neither a necessary nor a sufficient condition for a happy life.

During our holiday in Spain in the summer of 2018, we spent a week in an Airbnb villa in the forest adjacent to Nerja, a small town in southern Spain. The villa was on the top of a hill overlooking the Mediterranean Sea, and every evening we would sit on the terrace under the night sky watching the sea, the forest, the moon and the stars. My brother-in-law would bring out a couple of bottles of local wine and some cured meats. Our children would rustle up a salad, and then we would all munch and drink and take in the beauty around us. Dinner never tasted better than it did during those evenings in the forest.

On one such night, we saw a shooting star zip across the night sky. Twenty minutes later, we saw another shooting star, and then another. Until that evening, I had only read about shooting stars in Tintin comics. Seeing a shooting star is rare, and seeing three shooting stars in one evening is almost unheard of. If something as unlikely as that can happen, I thought, a middle-class professional launching a successful asset management business in India has to have a higher probability of success than I had imagined. Sitting under the starlit Spanish sky, I calculated the odds of my venture succeeding. I did something that I have done instinctively since high school—I considered the probability of success and multiplied it with the payoff that would kick in if the venture succeeded. Then I considered the probability of failure—which was significant, but not more than 50 per cent—and multiplied that with the financial downside that Sarbani and I would have to live with. Payoff from success less the financial downside was the number that crystallized in my head after I had watched the meteors fade away. The next morning, I called my friend and erstwhile executive assistant, Sudhanshu, in Mumbai and asked him to rent an office for our new, yet-to-be-named and yet-to-be-registered firm while I worked on the business plan sitting in Spain.

The next question was what to call the new firm. I came up with 'Katapult', but everyone else in the family thought that was a lame idea. I then suggested 'Invictus', and while that wasn't shot down immediately, I did not sense any groundswell of buy-in in our little house in the forest.

Muhammad Ali had been one of my heroes since I was a teenager. While I could never get his looks or his strength and power, I aspired to speak out like him in favour of causes that I believed in. In fact, it was exactly this trait of mine that used to rile my erstwhile colleagues and other powerful people in society at large.

To be more specific, what makes Muhammad Ali an utterly singular hero was his willingness to take a stance no one else in America at that point in time had the courage to take. David Remnick's Pulitzer Prize-winning biography *King of the World: Muhammad Ali and the Rise of an American Hero* (later made into a movie) captures the spirit of the great fighter and the era he dominated.[11]

Ali became the world champion in boxing in 1964. Then, in 1966, he refused to be drafted into the US military, citing his religious beliefs and opposition to the American involvement in Vietnam. Ali was arrested by the US authorities, found guilty of draft evasion and stripped of his titles by the World Boxing Federation. Refusing to bow down, Ali took the authorities to the Supreme Court, which overturned his conviction in 1971.

What followed was equally epic. Through the 1970s, Ali beat twenty-one boxers for the world heavyweight title and won fourteen unified title bouts. These records remained unbeaten for thirty-five years!

Remnick's book highlights that Ali's refusal to fight in the US Army in Vietnam—at least three years before it became fashionable for young Americans to take such a stance—was driven out of conviction rather than by a desire to look like a liberal. His belief in his convictions did not falter when the World Boxing Federation unlawfully stripped him of his titles and robbed him of his income at the peak of his career. He stood his ground and waited for the tide to turn, and when it did, he took what was rightfully his.

We named our firm Marcellus Investment Managers in honour of Cassius Marcellus Clay, better known as Muhammad Ali. This man's career, his beliefs and his actions inside and outside the boxing ring make him an inspiration for ordinary people like us who are trying to build something greater than ourselves with modest resources. For the team at Marcellus, whose investment philosophy and business model often pit us against the mainstream, the courage of Muhammad Ali's convictions is an ideal we aspire to.

In late July 2018, we returned from Europe to India, and I met my erstwhile colleague, Sudhanshu, who had for several years been my executive assistant. A qualified chartered accountant from one of the Big Four accounting firms, Sudhanshu had for many years helped me keep track of the business I had been managing. He had quit his job and agreed without hesitation to become the man who would help Marcellus keep track of its resources (which at that point were pitifully modest, i.e., Sarbani and my life's savings). Sudhanshu—who to this day knows exactly how much money we are earning, in which market and from what product—and I incorporated Marcellus Investment Managers in August 2018 and then applied to the Indian financial regulator for a licence to manage money. In the meantime, Sarbani, who is a graphic designer, designed the Marcellus logo with the batman-style 'M' and the Indian rupee sign as 'R' (that was actually our daughter Malini's idea).

We opened our doors to clients on 1 December 2018, and then watched as Marcellus took its initial baby steps. From its infancy, Marcellus showed promise, and then, when the COVID pandemic hit the toddler, the little firm rose to the challenge to emerge from the crisis stronger, not weaker. Today, we manage billions of dollars for many thousands of families across the world, alongside the monies of leading universities in the US and the UK.

Looking back and learning from the past

None of this would have happened had I not met Ana. My erstwhile employer did me a great favour by taking me down a path where a coach had to be brought in. In retrospect, I realize that until I met Ana, what I had been trying to do in those frustrating years was to pursue the sort of conventional corporate goals that conformist high achievers strive for. And yet, neither by upbringing nor by nature was I a conventional individual, a conventional thinker or a conventional leader. I was and remain a creative free thinker who is able to see the world in ways many others don't. This clash—between the way I behaved and thought on the one hand versus my hankering for a group CEO role in an investment bank (which is as conventional an aspiration as one can have in modern-day Mumbai) on the other—was creating tension and frustration for me, for my colleagues and for my family. The solution was to leave the conventional world of broking, money management and banking behind in order to pursue a life where I could not only do the things I liked—such as reading, writing, thinking and investing—but also work in an environment more conducive for free thinkers such as myself. Ana's coaching gradually helped me come to terms with this fact over the course of 2017 and 2018. Her coaching helped me find a new path—a path that ultimately led to the creation of Marcellus Investment Managers.

Helping incessantly-driven people like me understand how to not let their strengths become counterproductive is not easy for anyone. In retrospect, the way Ana did this was by giving me candid feedback through the coaching assignment—especially so in October 2017, when the feedback hit me like a sledgehammer. In short, Ana held up a mirror to my face and prompted me to reflect on the strengths and weaknesses of the person I saw in front of me. Left to myself, I would have said, '*I know I have weaknesses but so does everyone else. So let me just forge ahead in life.*' While there is a lot to be said for this approach when you are in the formative stages of your career, once you are in the boardroom, once you have power and influence, once you are responsible for a team, you need to understand yourself better. I strongly believe leaders need to understand their weaknesses and ensure that they don't damage themselves and the people around them.

If one critical part of coaching is feedback, the other equally important part is unconditional support and guidance from the coach. The coaching I received helped me break through the anger and confusion swirling in my head to understand what I really wanted from my career—namely, to build something that I deeply cared for, to do work that I really enjoyed and to find an outlet for my creative instincts. In effect, Ana helped me cut through the clutter and supported me in my realization that Marcellus had to be built. Ultimately, however, irrespective of the coach, one has to make one's own peace in this world; no one else can do that for us. While Ana helped me understand what my strengths and weaknesses were, it was left to me to figure out how to use my skillset—such as it was—to optimum effect in the context of a professional career that had run a relatively successful course but could do with a change in direction if I wanted a happier, more fulfilling life.

In order for the coaching to work, I had to trust Ana. However, as my colleagues had correctly pointed out in my feedback report, I am a naturally sceptical individual. Recognizing this, Ana invested heavily in building trust.

She has worked steadily and constantly—from our first meeting in the spring of 2017 in that coffee shop in London to the current day—to ensure that I understand that I had her unconditional support, no matter what happened in my corporate life.

Looking back at how working with Ana has helped me, I can identify two different strands in our coaching relationship:

- Reactive coaching: Here the client facing a specific challenge turns to the coach for advice on how to deal with it. My predicament in spring 2020 (with the COVID-19 pandemic not only hammering Marcellus's financial position but also forcing us to shut our offices) asked for this category of coaching. Ana responded in a way that showed understanding of the Marcellus leadership's state of mind (as all of us were working from home from various parts of India), crafting a session to bring us closer and make us more resilient. If we borrow an analogy from football, this is the sort of coaching that happens in the interval between the two halves.

- Proactive coaching: Here the coach uses her skillset to identify weaknesses in the client's toolkit or mental make-up. She then helps the client mitigate these weaknesses and, ideally, turn them into strengths. For example, Ana realized early on that a significant part of my own workaholism and my anxieties had their roots in the difficult financial circumstances in which I grew up in the UK. By helping me come to terms with the fact that that part of my life was behind me and should not continue to shape my thinking about the future, she was helping me deal with my difficult teenage years. To use a football analogy, this is the sort of coaching that takes place on the training ground weeks and months before match day. This is where a David Beckham practises hundreds of free kicks until he gets the curl and the swerve just right. This is where a Virat Kohli practises his forward defence until his head is perfectly still at the point of impact between bat and ball. In all forms of coaching, this is where the mind and body come together to help a leader become a better version of himself. The final issue highlighted in the closing paragraphs of the final chapter of this book is an example of proactive coaching at its most effective—here Ana applies a mental model that she understands really well and identifies a specific area in which I can get better.

What else has changed?

Leaving aside my quitting my job and setting up Marcellus, has anything else changed in my life as a result of the coaching? While a big part of me remains a 'work in progress' (we will focus on this in the closing chapters of this book), I can point to three sets of changes. First, I am spending more time with my family and with friends, although the COVID pandemic might deserve as much credit for this as my conscious efforts. As Sarbani told my parents in December 2021, '*The biggest positive that I can see from COVID is that Saurabh has slowed down a bit. Leaving aside the fact that he travels less due to COVID, he pushes himself a little less than he used to.*'

Second, I have become very conscious about external triggers that make me switch to hyperdrive at the workplace, which, in turn, brings out my stressors and triggers abrasive behaviour on my part. Dozens of chats with Ana over the years have made me recognize patterns in my behaviour that are early warning signals that I am about to go into hyperdrive and hence need to throttle off as soon as possible if I want to stop Dr Jekyll from becoming Mr Hyde. Throttling off might be as simple as powering down my laptop and going for a walk, or it might be the decision I took at the height of the pandemic panic in 2020 to hire a yoga trainer to help me improve my breathing and my ability to meditate to calm down my monkey brain. If I do fly off the handle, I make a note of it, and when Ana and I talk the next time, we dissect what happened, why it happened and what I can do to prevent a recurrence.

Third, while it has always been relatively easy for me to be empathetic towards people I like, I had in the past struggled to show empathy for people whose behaviours in the workplace were at odds with my view of what constitutes 'high-performance practices'. So, for a touchy-feely person in need of regular emotional reinforcement, historically I would not have been the leader to seek out. As I have seen the impact of Ana's coaching on how my mind works, I have realized that leadership is highly contextual. There are moments when I need to take on a leader-as-coach role. And while my wife teases me when she sees me reading *Emotional Intelligence* by Daniel Goleman (her point is that it's not going to happen for me!), thanks to being aware of the skills that I have less of, I have tried to put in place support systems for my colleagues. All of us have different strengths, and knowing our limitations and finding resources to complement our strengths profile is part of managing ourselves as leaders.

And finally, all of this stuff—touchy-feely as some of this may sound—helps me keep it together when the pressure to deliver, to generate returns for clients on the billions of dollars of assets under Marcellus's care, is at its most intense. As of 2022, Marcellus has been up and running for four years, and while those years have included the exhilarating post-March 2020 rally, they have also seen a vertiginous drop in the stock markets in January, February and March 2020. Those four years have also included several months when the COVID lockdown meant that we could not open our offices but still had to service the needs and deal with the queries of many thousands of clients from our home offices. Not once during those times of intense stress did I fly off the handle. When the pressure was at its highest, my years of coaching with Ana helped me stay calm, focused and with my rational mind ticking. My staying calm helps the rest of the Marcellus team stay calm. It also helps my family stay calm. When the loss of life from the pandemic was at its most intense in India in May and June 2021, our collective calm meant that we could provide support—practical, emotional and financial—and solace to our colleagues and their loved ones at their hour of greatest need. Leadership—by a group of people or by an individual—is needed most in times of crises, and it is in such circumstances that the most prepared minds can make the greatest difference.

Key Takeaways

- While I went into coaching with preconceived notions, I soon saw the value of the process, thanks to the reading material Ana shared with me at the start of our engagement. I got drawn into the wealth of research conducted by psychologists on productivity and creativity and what drives these types of qualities, both at the level of the individual and at the level of the team.

- Ana talked to my colleagues and my bosses to understand my personality better. Their feedback stung in a way no other feedback ever had. Further, Ana's Socratic style of questioning helped me understand my strengths and weaknesses, my likes and dislikes, and how I came across to those around me.

- As Ana started helping me build a picture of what I was and wasn't strong in, I began to realize that my desire to be the group CEO at my company was a waste of time and effort on my part.

- Two questions helped me choose the way forward—namely, 'What is the cause that I believe in?' and 'What is it that I enjoy?' To answer these questions, I went deep into my past. Ana's coaching sessions and her candid feedback made me realize that I needed to snap out of my mimetic desires and find and embrace my own underlying identity. I needed to become a person I was happy being.

- There were two different strands in our coaching relationship: reactive coaching (when the client asks the coach for specific help) and proactive coaching (when the coach identifies weaknesses and turns them into strengths).

In the clearing stands a boxer

And a fighter by his trade

And he carries the reminders

Of every glove that laid him down

And cut him 'til he cried out

In his anger and his shame

'I am leaving, I am leaving'

But the fighter still remains.

From the song 'The Boxer' by Paul Simon and Art Garfunkel (1969)

CHAPTER 4

A Leader's Hard-Won Lessons

Saurabh's reflections

The hardest thing about hard-won lessons is that they don't come cheap. In my case, behind each of my hard-won lessons is a story (usually involving a mistake or a sequence of mistakes) that I would prefer to forget. Over the past five years, as I have reflected on my discussions with Ana and on the reading material she has shared with me, I have gradually learnt to make fewer mistakes. As the reader will see in the penultimate chapter of the book, the coaching sessions per se are not where the lessons are actually learnt. Instead, the intensity of the discussions during the coaching session usually triggers a line of thought that opens up a new mental pathway or a new way of thinking. A few weeks later, sometimes months later, the penny drops and I hit upon a new, usually better, way of doing things. So here are the ten most valuable lessons I have learnt since I started working with Ana.

Lesson #1: Your most precious asset is your health

Let me go back to the closing months of 2016. I am on a Mumbai-to-London flight and we are taxiing down the runway at Heathrow towards Terminal 5. I gather my belongings and get ready for a quick dash to the next gate to catch a London to New York flight. However, upon landing at Heathrow, I find lengthy queues at the airport as the east coast of America is enveloped in a snowstorm and all flights from London to cities like New York, Boston, Washington D.C. and Philadelphia are cancelled.

What was supposed to be an hour-long layover at Heathrow becomes six hours of standing in various queues as I try to get on to a flight to a mid-western city in the US so that I can do my week-long trip there, as scheduled.

After an hour or so of standing in queues, I notice that my legs are giving away. My legs feel so weak that after another ninety minutes or so, I can barely stand straight. By the three-hour mark, I am sitting on the floor of the airport.

As I go through this experience, I reflect on how I got to this stage in my life. Until the time I turned thirty, I could run half-marathons with ease, and I ran the occasional 42-kilometre full marathon. Now here I am in Heathrow at the age of forty, barely able to stand up straight after nothing more exhausting than three hours of shuffling around in queues.

A week later, upon returning to Mumbai, I put myself through a full medical check-up followed by a visit to my GP. He explains that what has happened in the preceding five years is that my legs and the core of my body have gradually weakened because of lack of exercise. Five years of 400 flights a year have meant too much time sitting in a plane and too little time exercising. He recommends that I get a physiotherapist to start helping me get some of my strength back. For good measure, he tells me that I need to take fewer flights.

That's when I got my first reality check that the life that I was living was not sustainable. As I began my physiotherapy with a therapist—who was once physiotherapist to one of the Indian Premier League cricket teams—I started trying to figure out the rest of my life. That, in turn, led to the events that I have narrated to you in the preceding chapter.

In 2017, within a couple of months of beginning to coach me, Ana noticed that self-neglect was a recurrent pattern in my behaviour and she began highlighting this to me. That was the first time it dawned upon me that by damaging my health I was helping no one and achieving nothing. I realized later than I should have that pushing yourself and the people around you neither correlates with success nor with any sensible definition of leadership. In fact, as Ana gave me the 'sledgehammer feedback' referenced in the previous chapter, it struck me that one of the reasons I used to explode in front of my colleagues was because, by neglecting my health and by having a relentless travel schedule, I was burning my mental batteries out and therefore had no mental energy left for the more demanding discussions and negotiations that characterize corporate life.

As a result of Ana's inputs, from 400 flights a year I have managed to gradually bring my travel schedule down to around 100 flights a year. I have had a yoga trainer for the past couple of years. Besides three days of yoga and breathing exercises every week, I go to the gym twice a week. I have lost 4 kg in the past four years as I have cut down on my sugar, fat and red meat intake.

Lesson #2: Reflect deeply to understand your deepest/thickest desires and translate those desires into tangible outcomes (and let go of everything else)

As described in Chapter 3, within a few months of beginning coaching sessions with Ana in 2017, I became cognizant of my aspirations of becoming the group CEO at my erstwhile employer as not being the 'real me'. At that stage of my life, I was trying to become a person that really wasn't me—a wheeling, dealing, hustling banker who networks and schmoozes his way to success. The feedback that Ana gave me in the autumn of 2017 was the first time I really woke up to the consequences of trying to be—or pretending to be—a conventional finance professional and a Gordon Gekko-type leader. My subsequent discussions with Ana, with my wife Sarbani, with my friends and my erstwhile colleagues, made me see that to build a more sustainable life—a happier, healthier and more fulfilling life—I needed to go back to my roots and think about exactly what got my juices flowing. As described in Chapter 3, I spent the best part of a year reading and reflecting on this subject before founding Marcellus Investment Managers at the age of forty-two. Had I had a coach like Ana earlier on in my career, I am pretty sure I would have been compelled to confront these issues earlier too. The sooner we stop aping what we see in the world around us, the sooner we turn inwards and do what our deepest/thickest desires are pushing us to do, the sooner I reckon we will be on our way to building the lives and the careers that bring us satisfaction and happiness.

In our book *The Victory Project: Six Steps to Peak Potential*, my friend Anupam Gupta and I wrote about how to first find your deepest desire, and, second, to translate that desire into tangible outcomes.[1] The very first step ('Specialize') of our 'Simplicity Paradigm' starts with finding your deepest desire and specializing in that field. For many of us, the conflict between what we should do (to fulfil our deepest desires) and what we must do (because of financial or societal reasons) is the defining conflict of our lives. It doesn't have to be that way. It's taken me more than twenty years to understand that there is no conflict.

Through 2017 and 2018, as I read, discussed and thought about this issue in great detail, I realized that the trade-off people talk about (e.g., *You have to choose between a steady job and the financial security that comes with it versus the fluctuating fortunes of an entrepreneur*') is a false notion. You have neither financial nor emotional security if you are in a job you don't enjoy. There is no career advancement available for unhappy executives who churn out unimaginative slides/reports just for the pay cheque available at the end of the month. Specializing in what you love is the deepest fulfilment of your working career.

So, how does one find one's deepest desire? Robert Greene's book, *Mastery*, has a three-step method:[2]

Step 1: You must connect (or reconnect) with your inclinations, with your sense of uniqueness. In that regard, Step 1 focuses on looking inward—you search your past for signs of that inner voice. You try to clear away other voices—parents', friends', teachers'—that might confuse you. Greene says, *'You look for an underlying pattern, a core to your character that you must understand as deeply as possible.'*

Step 2: Having nailed Step 1, you look at the career path you are already on (or the one that you are about to begin following). The choice of this path is critical. More specifically, when you are choosing this career path, you need to avoid making needless distinctions between your professional and personal life. Greene says, '. . . you will need to enlarge your concept of work itself. Too often we make a separation in our lives— there is work and there is life outside work, where we find real pleasure and fulfilment.'

Step 3: Once you have figured out your career path, you need to give yourself a mental model of how your career will broadly pan out. Greene says:

> . . . you must see your career or vocational path more as a journey with twists and turns rather than a straight line. You begin by choosing a field or position that roughly corresponds to your inclinations . . . You don't want to start with something too lofty, too ambitious—you need to make a living and establish some confidence. Once on this path, you discover certain side routes that attract you, while other aspects of this field leave you cold. You adjust and perhaps move to a related field, continuing to learn more about yourself, but always expanding off your skill base.

One of the best examples of someone who found his deepest desire and then went on to achieve exceptional levels of mastery in that field is the veteran Indian investor Raamdeo Agrawal (or simply RA, as he is known), chairman and co-founder of Motilal Oswal Financial Services, a Mumbai-based investment management firm. Whereas most of us would visit restaurants simply to eat our meals and go about our day, RA would, at a young age, mentally recreate a financial ledger for the restaurant while eating. He would work out the number of customers, table turnarounds, average billings, etc., and construct a profit and loss (P&L) account within minutes. As if that wasn't enough, he would then have a friendly conversation with the owner to see if his calculations were accurate. This laid an early framework for RA to understand businesses. Not only did he get progressively better at analysing businesses but he also found that he loved the mental exercise of understanding the profitability of a business without being told what the revenues or costs were. It is when you do something that others find effortful—even difficult—but you find enjoyable, that you are connecting with your deepest desires and you are taking the first baby steps to mastery. This is the very expression of playing to one's strengths: registering rapid learning curves and feeling energized in the process.

With the benefit of hindsight, I can now identify when I took my first steps towards becoming an economist/analyst/ financial strategist/writer/investor. It was December 1991. My family had just moved to the UK and I was experiencing my first British winter. We didn't know too many people in London at that point and, financially and emotionally, it was a tough time for my parents and for my sister. I found a home away from home in the local library where I would read book after book. I devoured books written by Ernest Hemingway, James Joyce, Virginia Woolf, Herman Hesse, Salman Rushdie, V.S. Naipaul, Graham Greene, E.M. Forster, Gabriel Garcia Marquez, Ben Okri, Yukio Mishima, John Steinbeck and many more authors. In between reading books, to give myself a break, I would read the magazines kept in the library. That is how I came across a copy of *The Economist* for the first time, in December 1991. Once I figured that the weekly copy arrived in the library on Saturday mornings, every Saturday I would be the first visitor at the library.

On one such Saturday, I found an article in *The Economist* that was critical of India's handling of the situation in Kashmir. So, I sat in the library, took out my school notebook and wrote a letter to the editor of *The Economist* explaining why I thought the article did not capture the full picture of how Indians felt about the situation in Kashmir. Next Saturday morning, I found my letter in the magazine. In fact, just below my letter, *The Economist* had also published a rebuttal to it from the Pakistani High Commissioner to the UK who, not realizing that he was rebutting the point of view of a fifteen-year-old schoolboy, had taken a very strident tone and the high moral ground.

That was the first time I think I had a good laugh in those grim early months in London. That was the first time I noticed that my writing could make a difference. A year later, I got the prize for English in my local school in south London—the 'Grace Slaughter Prize for English' still occupies pride of place on our mantelpiece at home. And whenever I hear people sneer at intellectuals, thinkers and writers, I have a quiet chuckle and cast my mind back to my formative experiences as a thinker and writer.

Lesson #3: Invest emotionally in professional relationships but be objective about professional decisions

Through my thirties, as I gradually managed larger business, for understandable reasons, a variety of people—suppliers, colleagues and clients—tried to build closer relationships with me. However, I was still new to India and having spent my youth and the entirety of my twenties working in the UK, I found it hard to ascertain which relationships were being built with sincere intent and which ones might have an element of ulterior motive associated with them. As a result, I decided that I would not let anyone get close to me—my fear was that if they got close to me, they might take advantage of my proximity to them.

The headhunting firm that had been hired by my erstwhile employer to interview me and assess me picked up on this. This, in turn, was part of the briefing that they gave Ana when she began coaching me. Ana, in turn, gave me further feedback on this subject in the autumn of 2017.

It took me more than a year to fully comprehend the feedback that Ana had given me. In the early months of building Marcellus, when our financial resources were scarce and the small team was working long hours to build the business, I realized where I had been going wrong. As mentioned above, I had avoided investing emotionally in my closest professional relationships but in order to avoid hurting people, I had taken emotional professional decisions. For example, I let underperformers stay in my erstwhile firm for far longer than I should have.

As Marcellus's business gathered momentum, I knew that I needed to flip this paradigm, i.e., I needed to invest emotionally in my professional relationships, especially with my colleagues who were putting in everything they had towards creating Marcellus. At the same time, I needed to make objective decisions, day in and day out, 100 per cent of the time, not just about our investments but also about people, their compensation and their roles.

As a result, in Marcellus, my colleagues and I regularly head out in the evening to play cricket matches under floodlights on Friday evenings (followed by pizza and other indulgent snacks). The entire firm heads to the countryside or to a resort for a weekend outing every six months. There are monthly lunches for the whole firm and there is a birthday cake-cutting day every month (to celebrate that month's birthday girls and boys).

However, when it comes to difficult decisions, I hold my nerve and try my best to take an objective, rather than an emotional, stance. For example, in 2019, a young, hard-working employee did something that was unethical. Marcellus's operations team spotted this and reported the matter to me. I requested HR to look into the matter. The recommendation from HR was that the youngster should be asked to leave. I acted upon the same recommendation immediately.

Lesson #4: Allocate responsibilities, set the guardrails for performance and then ask your colleagues the right questions

In most white-collar jobs, in the formative years of our careers—usually when we are in our twenties—we get rewarded for having more knowledge and skills than others. If you are, as I was, a management consultant or an equity analyst, the more mental models you can build in your twenties, the more companies and industries you are able to understand by the time you turn thirty, and the better you will do in your career (all other things being equal).

Partly because of my own tendency to read lots of material and partly because of the training programmes in the firms I worked in through my twenties, I became an expert at learning new mental models and gaining knowledge about new companies and industries. As I stepped into my thirties and as my managerial responsibilities grew, I did not recognize that I now needed a very different skill set to succeed. Specifically, I did not realize—until Ana began coaching me the year I turned forty—that I was no longer in a position to provide readymade solutions to the business problems faced by my direct reports; my job was now to understand what my colleagues were doing and ask the right questions.

More generally, I understood that as we evolve from being focused subject-matter experts in our twenties to managers in charge of teams and leaders of entire departments and businesses in our thirties, we can no longer be the master of everything we survey. It is simply not possible for the same person to be, for example, a legal and compliance expert, a tech and operations expert and a finance expert. Finance, compliance and technology are vast domains by themselves, and as a leader, I must empower talented, able professionals to get the job done far better than

I will be able to. So, what would be my job in the context of finance, compliance and technology? Foremost, I must ask the right questions and supply the necessary resources to help my team to perform, deliver and feel motivated at the same time. The 'Leader as Coach' is an important aspect of leadership, and my own experience with coaching has certainly highlighted the importance of curiosity and asking powerful questions when it comes to raising the performance of the business I work in.

And what exactly are the 'right questions'? As we built Marcellus, I found three types of questions to be particularly useful when I meet my direct reports.

The first type is 'Completeness Questions'. For example, if we are reviewing Marcellus's technology-and-IT budget for the next financial year, I will ask my team in tech and ops whether we have thought about what tech support our US sales team will need, what systems our traders will need, what trade monitoring systems our compliance team will require and what financial data our analysts will want to buy.

The second type is 'Think Differently Questions': for example, if we are reviewing our office space budget for the next financial year, I need to ask, given how many of our colleagues now prefer to work from home, whether we need one desk per Marcellus employee or 0.7 desks per Marcellus employee. As we explore these questions together, I don't necessarily know whether the correct number is 0.7 or 0.9, but unless I ask these questions of my colleagues in HR, we are not tapping into our full thinking resources and I am not doing my job properly as a leader.

The third type is 'Are We Focusing on The Right Things?' questions. For example, whenever a client asks me, '*Should I invest with Marcellus?*', my response is, '*What would you like your equity portfolio to do?*' or '*What are your investment goals?*' Only if a client is clear in his head about his investment goals (e.g., '*I would like to retire in fifteen years*'; '*I would like to send my kids to study abroad in ten years' time*') do I get into the discussion around '*Is a Marcellus product appropriate for you?*' All of us—including myself, when I am under pressure—tend to respond to difficult situations by ignoring the real question (which usually takes heavy-duty mental processing to answer) and focusing on a relatively easier question. My job as a leader in such situations is to keep everyone's focus on the difficult questions.

Questions are a means for a leader to tap into the unique ability that human beings have: the ability to collaborate. We can cooperate in extremely flexible ways with a countless number of strangers, as Yuval Noah Harari wrote in *Sapiens*.[3] Almost every product we see and use, indeed our relationships, are born of collective effort. For example, the writing of this book is a form of collaboration not just between the two authors but also the editors and reviewers of this book and the several people whose interviews form the basis of the next chapter of this book.

To say 'collaboration is important for leaders to bring out the best in their teams' might sound like stating the obvious. However, this 'obvious' point is not well-received wisdom in many business circles. If you take the books written by and about great corporate leaders like Steve Jobs, Jack Welch and J.P. Morgan, they usually focus on how the leader made important judgement calls at critical junctures and thus took his people to the promised land. While this 'leader as hero' paradigm makes for a good movie script, in most contemporary companies, the levels of complexity of the business are such that no one person can be the all-knowing, all-seeing, all-powerful, all-action hero steering the ship.

Lesson #5: Aim for an environment of 0 per cent politics, 0 per cent friction and 100 per cent collaboration

Through my thirties, I read several books written by (or about) hard-charging American corporate leaders like Jack Welch,[4] Lee Iacocca[5] and Louis Gerstner.[6] One of the lessons I took away from these books is that I needed to create a competitive environment within my team so that everyone understood that the highest performers—those on the right tail of the bell curve that HR professionals loved to stack people up on after performance appraisals—will get the biggest rewards. I learnt the hard way that this is a seriously bad idea that can damage people's careers, their personal lives and entire companies.

Around a decade or so ago, as the business I was managing at that time grew rapidly, I knew that I would need to spend more time meeting clients across the world. Hence, I announced to several of my direct reports that one of them would have to take charge of a large part of my internal responsibilities as I ran around in India and the rest of the world signing up clients. The good news was that most of my direct reports were highly capable, industrious, ambitious professionals. The bad news was that two of them were super-driven and both wanted the job because of everything it represented—more money, more status and more power within the team. My decision thus triggered a civil war between these two men, who until that point had been best friends.

As these two gents politicked to get promoted, their performance suffered. They forced most people in the team to take sides—'either you are with me, or you are with him'. The youngsters in the team were both captivated by this corporate slugfest and at the same time terrified that their careers might become a casualty of this rivalry.

It ended as all such gladiatorial corporate contests end—one of the two men got promoted, and thanks to the rancour and the bad blood created by the contest, the other man left the firm. My colleague who quit was one of the most talented people I have met in my professional career. Like the colleague who got promoted, the colleague who left has gone on to enjoy enormous success in India over the past decade. The real loser was the team and the firm—we needlessly lost a highly talented, high-performing professional by creating a contest where none should have existed.

Teams and companies are usually focused on one collective goal. The notion that for 364 days in the year, a company can make its employees focus on a collective goal and then on the 365th day conduct performance appraisals that measure employees relative to each other (and then go on to reward them relative to each other) seems foolish, as it undermines collaboration and camaraderie within the team. Rather than making the team more than a sum of its parts, talented professionals are made to feel like virtuoso performers rather than members of a high-quality orchestra.

When Marcellus was created five years ago, we were determined to avoid this pitfall. The first thing to go was the bell curve or any other performance management system which says that team members' performance must be measured relative to each other's. In businesses like ours where, to make the customer happy, every single part of the business has to fire in unison and in perfect co-ordination, it is illogical for me to say to one colleague, *'We have had a great year and you are in the 90th percentile of our bell curve but your colleague in the adjacent department is in the 60th percentile and will therefore get a much smaller bonus than you will.'* You can imagine that the 90th percentile performer in sales will be looking at the 60th percentile performer and thinking, *'I owe my success to the guy who is the 60th percentile performer. This year I got a nice bonus, and he got a raw deal, but how sustainable is my big bonus if the people I depend on are getting a raw deal?'*

Inspired by what Peter Thiel has said on this subject, the second thing I spent time figuring out in the opening months of creating Marcellus was how each member of the management team would have only one job, and that job would be unique to that person. As a result, there would be neither duplication of responsibilities nor competition between colleagues. The focus would be on outgunning the competition rather than your colleagues in the firm.

Learning from what the American fund manager Ray Dalio has said in his book *Principles,*[7] the third thing I did was to request two of my colleagues—who are not founders of Marcellus—to write a compensation document that would define how all of us would get paid, how the bonus pot would be calculated at the end of the year, how it would be split among the leadership team members and how the process would be completely transparent; i.e., every single member of the leadership team would be able to see what every other person is getting paid. After these two colleagues had written the document, I requested them to seek feedback from the rest of Marcellus's management and from Marcellus's shareholders. Perhaps because I had made minimal inputs for this ten-page compensation document, determining rewards in Marcellus has so far been a relatively smooth process, bereft of the year-end acrimony that I had got so accustomed to in my previous job.

Lesson #6: Create 'circuit breakers' (or systems and processes) that prevent you from being your own worst enemy

After I went through the physical breakdown described at the beginning of this chapter, I hired a physiotherapist, Dr Jimit, to help me regain my strength and fitness. Having helped professional cricketers regain their fitness, Dr Jimit knew what exercises I needed to do. After a couple of sessions, we had established a neatly laid-out sequence of exercises that I was supposed to execute daily. I purchased the necessary exercise equipment from Amazon—a yoga mat, some elastic bands, light weights, etc.—and was keen as mustard to stick to my new fitness regime. However, there was one problem—finding the time to exercise.

Since I used to leave for work at 7.15 a.m., the only way I could get an hour of exercise into my daily schedule was to wake up at 5 a.m. However, since I used to get home from work at 9 p.m., it would be 11 p.m. by the time I fell asleep. That, in turn, meant I used to struggle to wake up at 5 a.m., which, in turn, meant that I wasn't getting much exercise done. So, how was I going to regain my fitness?

Fortunately for me, around this time, prompted by a newspaper review of Charles Duhigg's blockbuster bestseller *The Power of Habit*,[8] I purchased the book. I learnt from the book that over the past twenty years, psychologists have not only discovered that our habits are far more influential than we understood them to be but also that they are *not* controlled by the 'thinking' part of our brain.[9]

Advances in science have now helped us understand how habits (or the 'habit loop') work in a three-step framework. Sequentially, these are:

1. **A cue**: This is a trigger (something you see, smell or hear) that transfers the brain into an automatic mode which determines which habit to use;
2. **A routine**: This is the heart of the habit and is typically a mental, emotional or physical routine;
3. **A reward**: This helps the brain ascertain if this specific loop is worth remembering for the future.

Duhigg says, '*The cue and reward become neurologically intertwined until a sense of craving emerges.*'

Learning from Duhigg, I implemented a system that helps me wake up at 5 a.m. every weekday morning and get my exercise regime going. When I wake up, I have my running shoes close to the bed. That is my cue that I need to get some exercise. That cue triggers a routine of my putting on my gym clothes, going down to the gym and working out. Throughout this process, I need a reward that keeps me going through the dark Mumbai mornings (accompanied by heavy rain from June to September). My reward is a peanut butter sandwich with jam layered on top for breakfast. My wife ensures that I won't get the sandwich if I don't go to the gym. That's how my exercise habit loop works.

While my 'jam and toast' for breakfast is an example of a simple but useful 'rule' that helps me in my personal life, similar rules, systems and processes have proved to be equally useful to me in my professional life.

As explained in previous chapters, when I was the CEO at my erstwhile employer, I had a habit of losing my temper under pressure. When Ana began coaching me, she took feedback from my direct reports on this trait of mine. Ana and I then discussed the circumstances in which I tended to lose my temper (or 'amygdala hijacks', as Ana labelled them). In between leaving my previous job and setting up Marcellus, I reflected on my temper tantrums and my discussions with Ana on this subject. I became aware that these blow-ups tended to happen often towards the fag end of the day— usually when I was tired after burning out my mental batteries. Often these blow-ups involved company politics, usually with money at the heart of the matter. Sometimes, these discussions involved appraisals of and bonus payments to various team members.

It became clear that if I could replicate my 'jam and toast' example in my professional life, I could reduce the incidence of my temper tantrums. So, I put three 'circuit breakers' in place to reduce the probability of amygdala hijacks. The first circuit breaker was the rules-based bonus allocation system that I have discussed earlier in this chapter, at the end of lesson 3.

The second was a shareholders' agreement, which was created to tie all of Marcellus's founding team into a mutually reinforcing set of powers and obligations. For example, on all matters relating to how Marcellus spent its cash, most of the founders—by number—would have to sign off. No one founder, including me, has the power to use Marcellus's funds at his whim and fancy. I also decided that whenever possible, discussions with my fellow founders on difficult subjects are best done in the first half of the day, when our mental batteries are fully charged.

Third, I was acutely conscious that while in my previous firm I had several senior people ten and fifteen years older than me deal with my amygdala hijacks and calm me down, in Marcellus I was the oldest employee (which meant that there would be little to no calming influence if I blew my top). Sitting in the forest in Spain in the summer of 2018, I knew that we needed a senior statesman or stateswoman to guide my fellow founders and me through the ups and downs that Marcellus would inevitably encounter. Given that a start-up in any country is a high-pressure work environment with long working hours and all sorts of financial constraints, the last thing any of my colleagues needed was temper tantrums from me. My colleague Sudhanshu and I began the hunt for a wise person with grey hair whom we hoped would hold our hand in our darkest hours.

We began by creating a shortlist on an Excel spreadsheet of the half dozen men and women that we knew could perform this role. Looking at the list, we understood that these people had all reached such senior positions in the corporate world that we had no hope in hell of being able to compensate them with consultancy fees—the 'day rate' for these gurus would be astronomically high. Hence, we decided that in return for their wisdom and handholding, we would offer them a small stake in the firm.

I then sent emails to these six men and women and explained that we were setting up Marcellus and were looking for an external investor who would take a small stake in the firm and act as a guide. With nothing else to do at that juncture, I went back to writing *The Victory Project*, the book I referenced earlier in this chapter. Within hours of my sending out the emails, Mohandas Pai (known now to everyone at Marcellus as 'MDP'), the former chief financial officer, then head of HR and director of an iconic IT services company in Bengaluru, responded saying that he was flying to Mumbai (from Bengaluru) that evening and would like to meet us. He wrote that since he would be busy with meetings all the next day, the only slot he had for us was upon landing in Mumbai. We agreed to meet at 10 p.m. that night at Mumbai airport.

There we were—Sudhanshu and I—standing at the 'Arrivals' gate at Mumbai airport on a rainy monsoon evening in 2018. We soon spotted the tall, commanding figure that is MDP. Unfortunately for us, he had exited from the airport through an alternative gate, and upon not finding us there had become irritated. *'This isn't going well,'* I thought, as I ushered MDP towards the Starbucks in front of the airport. We took a corner table and Sudhanshu took out our business plan slide deck. MDP was not interested in the deck. He asked us three simple questions—What are you guys trying to do? How will you go about doing it? What does success mean for you?

It took us around thirty minutes to answer these questions. MDP, dressed in his trademark Indian kurta, listened attentively while I cursed myself for having worn a pair of faded jeans and a cotton T-shirt to the meeting. Half an hour into the meeting, he said, '*I will take a stake in Marcellus and do whatever I can to help you.*' Sudhanshu and I looked at each other, speechless. We offered to take him through the slides we had prepared. He then offered us the first of the many lessons we have received from him.

He said, '*Saurabh, business relationships are fundamentally based on trust, not on PowerPoint. I have met you a couple of times before. I trust you to do the right thing. I can see that you guys have a plan. It is a simple plan, but I think it makes sense. I know this industry well and have done extensive work on the asset management business model before. If changes must be made to it, we will make them in due course. At this juncture, you need to get on with it and incorporate the company, get a licence from SEBI, get an office and build the team.*' And that was that. Even before we had drained our coffee cups, MDP had finished the meeting and had headed off towards his hotel. As I saw him and his chauffeur walk towards the car park that monsoon night, I promised myself that I would train myself to build such 'insane' clarity of thought on what, to most mortals, would be a complicated judgement call.

In the months that followed, MDP's family office took a stake in Marcellus, attributing to the firm a valuation that many others would say we did not deserve at that juncture (this was a year prior to Marcellus hitting profitability). As Marcellus blossomed and as other investors from various parts of the world approached Marcellus with all sorts of offers (e.g., give us a stake and we will open up this or that geographical market for you), MDP remained an outstanding sounding board for us. Whenever we missed a beat in how we planned and plotted Marcellus's future, MDP would remind me of my new avatar: '*Saurabh, you need to stop thinking like an equity analyst and start thinking like an owner of a business.*'

In a world full of uncertainty, habits and circuit breakers, gurus like MDP and coaches like Ana give us the best chance of overcoming our weaknesses and putting the best bits of our personality to optimal use.

Lesson #7: Prepare meticulously for internal meetings with colleagues

In autumn 2017, when Ana visited Mumbai and sat in on several of my meetings with my direct reports, she pointed out that in most internal meetings, I was doing most of the talking. Implicitly, she nudged me towards realizing that since these were my direct reports, they should be doing more of the talking in the meetings, given that they were either briefing me on how they were managing their responsibilities or telling me about the challenges they were facing.

Upon receiving this feedback, I tried to respond to it by speaking less in meetings but then found that that by itself didn't work. So, I spent a few months ruminating on what the underlying problem was. In the intervening months between quitting my job and starting Marcellus, I hit upon the core issue, namely, because I was running around so much meeting clients across the world, I wasn't preparing properly for meetings. Since I was going into internal meetings with colleagues unprepared, a big chunk of the time in the meeting was taken by me in understanding and clarifying the matter at hand. That, in turn, meant there wasn't enough time spent in the meeting brainstorming solutions and agreeing upon the way forward. Unfortunately, that created the need for yet another meeting (say, the subsequent week) which, in turn, meant that my schedule got rammed even tighter. And thus the cycle continued year after year until Ana spotted that something was awry.

So, when Marcellus was in its infancy, I hit upon a way to break this cycle. I now schedule all important meetings with the firm's leadership or, say, appraisals or monthly check-ins with my direct reports at least a fortnight in advance. I then put the agenda of the meeting in the meeting invite and either provide background material or seek briefing material well in advance. Ahead of the meeting, I ensure that I read the material carefully and the day prior, I spend time thinking through how the meeting will pan out. What sort of issues or roadblocks are we likely to hit in the meeting? Is there a psychological issue lurking under the surface of the meeting that I need to understand? Is there a knotty business problem that I need to think through? For example, if we are struggling to fill a specific senior role in the firm, should I call a friend ahead of the meeting who can give me useful inputs on the subject (e.g., a headhunter who specializes in hiring senior managers in that sector)?

Once the meeting begins, I sit back and listen for as long as possible as my colleagues give their inputs on the problem at hand. Since all of us have read the same briefing material coming into the meeting, the meeting rapidly becomes focused on solutions and the way forward. Given the quality of the talent in Marcellus, the solutions usually come from the team at large. In the rare instance that my colleagues are stumped, I amp up my mental intensity and explain how in my two decades of managing businesses similar to Marcellus I have seen similar problems getting resolved.

I have found that this mode of working confers several benefits. For starters, my colleagues grow their skill sets faster as each meeting becomes a mini business case exercise in a relatively low-risk internal setting. Secondly, as their confidence grows and as their autonomous control of their business unit increases, it frees me up to do what I enjoy most: think about the big-picture strategic challenges and about the firm's investments in totality across our burgeoning client base. And thirdly, this mode of management means that my mental batteries do not get depleted on a regular basis.

Lesson #8: Give yourself and your colleagues time and space (rather than pushing yourself or them more)

It was a pleasant January evening in Mumbai and I was attending a client's son's wedding in the northern suburbs of the city. The wedding was being hosted on the lawns of a nice hotel and I remember, at this very pleasant engagement, standing in the middle of the lawns with a drink in my hand. It was early 2018 and I was in the middle of my first coaching stint with Ana. As I mingled with the guests at the wedding, I bumped into a couple of ex-colleagues who used to be my direct reports. As we exchanged pleasantries, it struck me that both my ex-colleagues, who were in their thirties, looked fresher and fitter than I had seen them before. I asked them what the secret of their new, improved, youthful look was. For half a minute there was silence, and a couple of awkward glances were exchanged between my ex-colleagues. Then they explained that while working for me, they had been pushed so hard that they had no time to go to the gym and ended up spending twelve hours of the day working. Because they used to spend so much time under pressure in the office, they would end up consuming endless amounts of tea and coffee (which in India is inevitably heavily sugared), while snacking and smoking alongside. The result was expanding waistlines and falling levels of energy, even as I, blissfully unaware of all this, ramped up the pressure to deliver.

After getting this download from my ex-colleagues, I lost my appetite for dinner that evening. I proceeded to congratulate the newlyweds and then headed home to contemplate what my hard-charging management style had done to able men and women in the prime of their careers. Speaking to Ana in the months and years that followed, the realization dawned on me that pushing people relentlessly rarely results in positive outcomes. There will be times when the *Titanic* is going down, and in a 'fight or flight' scenario, you have to ramp up the adrenaline rapidly to help your colleagues and yourself, but such circumstances should be the exception rather than the norm. In fact, if such circumstances are the norm and you are fighting fires every day, then there is something seriously wrong with your business and beating up the team isn't going to solve it.

Discussing this subject with Ana through 2020 as my colleagues and I tried to keep Marcellus growing through the COVID-19 pandemic yielded another layer of insights into the area of when to push the team and when to hold back.

Like much of the rest of the world, from late March 2020 onwards, we were locked down at home. In fact, March 2020 had been doubly difficult for us. Not only were we forced to shut our office and work from home, but our performance fees too, which at that time accounted for the bulk of our revenues, were almost entirely wiped out by the COVID-induced stock market crash of March 2020. There we were in April and May 2020, sitting at home with Marcellus's financial reserves going down, with the office shut, and therefore with little or no ability to sign up new business. It was easy to make out on the Zoom calls that morale among the Marcellus team was running low. I remember writing to Ana in early June 2020 saying that this was a fight or flight scenario and that I felt that I needed to rally the troops as the pandemic swept across the world. That was when Ana offered to do a collective Zoom call with the Marcellus leadership. I spoke to my colleagues about her offer, and we decided then that getting Ana to moderate a discussion among ourselves would be extremely helpful.

On that Zoom call, Ana asked each of us to do a couple of seemingly simple exercises, such as each one talking about a difficult time in our lives. She also asked us to say what we admired most in our colleagues (Ana did not allow us to waffle; we had to be specific. For example, we had to say something like, *'What I really admire about XYZ is that he is considerate and takes on more than his fair share of calls with difficult clients'*). I could literally see the pressure levels abating on that Zoom call as my colleagues, scattered across different parts of India in the third month of the COVID-19 lockdown, felt and expressed greater empathy for each other than they had ever before.

After that call, Ana and I debriefed. Without her telling me in as many words, I understood that there was no point in rallying the troops at this juncture. The pandemic and the lockdown were sapping their emotional reserves as they focused on helping their families and friends deal with the shutting down of schools, the loss of livelihood and, most tragically, the loss of lives. I knew I had to focus on helping the Marcellus team come out of this disaster with as few mental and emotional scars as possible. Rome could be built after COVID-19 had passed.

Inspired by what Ana had helped me understand, I delved further into the subject—of how I could build emotional strength and mental focus to attain success in difficult circumstances. Here are the four principles that I have found immensely useful:

Principle 1: Frugality. Not buying or owning things that add very little to your life not only saves you money but also frees up mind space for more useful activities. I don't believe in buying the latest smartphone every year and I don't believe in stocking up on clothes and shoes at sales. I have at any point in time owned one suit, six shirts (one for each working day of the week) and one pair of shoes. As a result, not only is my closet empty, my decision as to what to wear to work requires no application of mind. I wear these items until they wear out, regardless of what the latest trend in men's fashion might be.

Principle 2: Positivity. Thanks to what Ana has helped me learn, and also reinforced by my research, I am now a hardcore believer in positivity. When dealing with my emotions, especially my fears and anxieties (of which there are many), I try to follow a constructive, level-headed approach. Research tells us that the brain is: (a) incredibly sensitive to positive suggestions, and (b) suffers from 'confirmation bias' with regard to our preconceived notions about ourselves. This wiring of the human brain is a potent driver of self-improvement, and I try to tap into this without letting my workaholic tendencies take over.

Principle 3: Reduction of clutter to improve focus. Focus helps us connect our practice with our purpose and our execution with our vision. I declutter with zeal. Especially on weekdays, I strip away everything that diverts my attention from work. There are two specific practices that help me: one, avoiding 'networking events'; and two, ruthlessly controlling the content I consume on my phone and on my laptop. I have no Twitter or Instagram accounts and I don't have WhatsApp on my phone or on my computer. Ultimately, these two practices significantly improve the time I get to do deliberate, focused, deep work.

Principle 4: Daily meditation. Meditation is a practice where an individual trains her attention to achieve a clear, calm and stable state of mind. The Dalai Lama believes that meditation and prayer have similar benefits. However, my reading on the subject suggests that there are two differences between meditation and prayer. Firstly, meditation is, in general, a more advanced form of concentrating and focusing the mind than prayer. Secondly, while prayer has as its focus either a god or a deity, meditation—especially in its more advanced forms— can be about completely blanking out the mind (which sounds easy but is very difficult to do). The benefits of meditation— going from the most basic to the most advanced practice of it— appear to be stress relief and recovery from difficult experiences, clarity of thought and greater focus, higher levels of thinking and creativity, and greater ability to work cooperatively.

Lesson #9: Be on the lookout for exceptionally curious people

During my teenage years and into my twenties, like other ambitious youngsters, I was very focused on building my credentials through the appropriate educational and professional qualifications from suitably prestigious institutions. Then, after I had spent a decade or so working in India, I noticed that a lot of very successful businesspeople in India did not have these credentials (nor did they care about having such credentials). For a few years, I was puzzled by this—'*How can you run a large business without any sort of educational or professional credentials?*' I thought.

In parallel, in my erstwhile firm, I became very focused on hiring the best talent that I could afford with the best credentials. Then, as the years went by, I saw that the success rate of the most credentialed professionals is not significantly higher than those of less qualified people. In fact, the professionals from the most prestigious universities tended to create more management issues for me than others who were just as productive but did not have the backstop of having an Indian equivalent of an Ivy League education.

As Ana and the headhunting firm gave me feedback in autumn 2017 on my areas for development, I noticed a pattern in their feedback. While issues around self-neglect and anger management were areas I needed to rectify, I noticed in the feedback that I scored highly on 'curiosity'. As I dwelled further on this point, I realized that the underlying trait I needed to look for in people—both team members and the CEOs of the companies that we invested in—is exceptional levels of curiosity. So, why is 'curiosity' so powerful?

In fast-growing and rapidly changing economies like India, the core trait that helps professionals attain enduring success is the hunger to understand: (a) how the world is changing, (b) what is driving the specific changes in the industry they work in, and (c) how they can help their business capitalize on these changes.

Curious professionals not only ask such questions more often than less curious people (who might be more qualified from an academic perspective), curious professionals also push themselves harder to find answers to such questions. And because such professionals have behaved like this for extended periods of time, their mental fortitude and intellectual stamina tend to be greater. That, in turn, allows them to keep working hard to solve difficult problems long after others have given up. This explains why many of the builders of India's greatest companies do not have prestigious qualifications but are exceptionally good at solving difficult business problems.

Thanks to this insight, when we built Marcellus, provided the applicants' qualifications passed basic levels of hygiene for that role, we increasingly ignored the qualifications of applicants. Instead, we create a series of case questions focused on helping us understand how much our prospective colleagues read, what sort of material they read, what sort of podcasts they listen to, how they seek to constantly upgrade their skill sets and how they apply this knowledge to practical business situations. So, for example, when we interview analysts, we often give them the last ten years of annual reports on a listed company and tell them to identify the most critical business issue faced by the said company which, if solved, will transform the company's fortunes. We tell our prospective colleague that she can take as long as she wants to read the annual reports, to understand the business and research it in-depth before she answers the question.

When it comes to tackling open-ended business problems such as these, we have found that curious professionals are significantly more successful than credentialed professionals. This insight has helped me build a far stronger team at Marcellus than I have ever been able to build before.

Lesson #10: Learn to communicate as clearly as possible to both internal and external audiences

As discussed in the previous chapter, I learnt to write clearly while I was in school in the UK. Then, in my early twenties, I was extremely fortunate to work under a manager at Accenture, Steve Norton, who drilled into my head how to write a tightly worded business memo. Steve did me a big favour by introducing me to Barbara Minto's Pyramid Principle of communication wherein the most efficient method of communicating a message or a point of view is:

- You begin by stating the 'Situation', i.e., the common point of view or knowledge that you and the audience share;
- You then state the 'Complication', i.e., the issue at hand or the 'burning platform' issue about which the audience is worried;
- You then state the 'Question' that the audience wants answered or the business problem that the audience wants a solution for; and
- Finally, you state the 'Answer' or the solution.

This simple but very effective format of communication is called 'Situation-Complication-Question-Answer' or S-C-Q-A in short. When I started working in the stock market in London at the age of twenty-six, I successfully adapted SCQA and used it to pitch stocks both through emails, on the phone and in face-to-face meetings. So, the twenty-six-year-old Saurabh would pitch to fund managers twice as old as him by saying:

- (Situation) As you know, economic growth is healthy and well-managed British lenders are growing their loan books and their profits at a healthy rate.
- (Complication) But the problem is that all of these lenders are trading at expensive valuations.
- (Question) So, the challenge for investors is to find a way to profit from the underlying growth in the economy without having to buy overvalued stocks?
- (Answer) One way to do that is to buy XYZ lender. This lender has been around for over a century. During that time, the said firm has shown steady growth in profits by focusing on small-ticket lending in niche markets in northern England. Since the firm is operating in an unsexy part of the lending market and since the management doesn't bother promoting the firm in the media, the stock is trading at very reasonable valuations.

SCQA worked nicely for my colleagues and myself in India as well. However, as I became more senior and as my management responsibilities in my previous job grew, I didn't realize that I needed to find an equally compelling way to communicate internally with my colleagues. As I neglected to communicate clearly and frequently with the 100+ analysts, salespeople, traders, accountants and operations staff in the business, a messaging vacuum was created. Some of my colleagues filled up this vacuum with messages they wanted to communicate (which were not necessarily the messages I wanted to communicate). So, while laying the foundations of Marcellus, I was determined not to let this happen again.

From the week that Marcellus received its license to manage money, I created a cycle of meetings that has served us well so far, namely:

- Every Monday at 8.30 a.m., the whole firm meets via a video-call to agree upon execution priorities for the week ahead. The agenda for the Monday Morning Meeting (MMM) is agreed on the Friday prior. I chair the meeting, but most of the agenda items are led by the respective divisional heads and the managers reporting to them. I note down action points and the deadlines associated with them are emailed to the whole firm within minutes of the MMM ending. Since everyone in Marcellus knows that the action points in week t will be part of the agenda of the MMM in week t+1, all our minds are focused on ensuring that the execution agenda is actioned expeditiously.
- Every month, the entire leadership of the firm meets for half a day to discuss strategic and operational issues facing the firm or opportunities that are shaping up and that might warrant decisive action on our part. I collate the agenda for such meetings a week prior and share it with my colleagues. Once again, action points from the meeting are circulated to the leadership expeditiously and any points not actioned in the subsequent month are then discussed again a month later.
- Once every quarter, we discuss Marcellus's financial progress with the firm as a whole. Our finance team presents the numbers. The leadership highlights both areas in which we are progressing well and areas that need additional work. Since a third of Marcellus's employees also have an equity

interest in the firm, this also doubles up as a discussion among the major shareholders of the firm.

- Once every six months, we go through an appraisal cycle where every manager seeks detailed feedback from the broader firm on his direct reports and then provides both verbal and written feedback to his direct reports. As part of this semi-annual feedback cycle, I spend a week in September and then another week in March taking feedback from a variety of people across the firm (most of whom are not my direct reports). Then I sit down with my direct reports to discuss the feedback.

This calendar of pre-planned internal meetings and discussions keeps Marcellus broadly on track. As the firm grows, we have our fair share of business and operational issues to contend with. What this calendar does is allow us to spot issues as they arise and then collaborate in a methodical manner to address the challenge at hand. That, in turn, minimizes the scope for messaging vacuums and the corporate politics that usually accompany such vacuums.

Could I have learnt these lessons earlier?

As Ana and I were writing this book, I often wondered if I could have learnt the lessons highlighted in this chapter earlier in my career. For example, could a thirty-year-old Saurabh have trained himself to build great teams where there is minimal friction and politics and drive high performance through Socratic questioning? I don't think so.

Learning how to manage your own health, your own workload and stressors, and learning how to manage large groups of talented professionals is not something that you and I can get from a course. A big part of growing and developing as a leader consists of making difficult decisions, then suffering the consequences (if your decisions are not correct) and then learning from those mistakes. However, with the benefit of hindsight, I think the process of learning can be made a little quicker and a bit less painful by learning from others who have walked these paths before and by having a coach who has seen other leaders deal with these situations before.

Key Takeaways

Lesson #1: Your most precious asset is your health.

Lesson #2: Reflect deeply to understand your deepest/thickest desires and translate those desires into tangible outcomes (and let go of everything else).

Lesson #3: Invest emotionally in professional relationships but be objective about professional decisions.

Lesson #4: Allocate responsibilities, set the guardrails for performance and then ask your colleagues the right questions.

Lesson #5: Aim for an environment of 0 per cent politics, 0 per cent friction and 100 per cent collaboration.

Lesson #6: Create 'circuit breakers' (or systems and processes) that prevent you from being your own worst enemy.

Lesson #7: Prepare meticulously for internal meetings with colleagues.

Lesson #8: Give yourself and your colleagues time and space (rather than pushing yourself or them more).

Lesson #9: Be on the lookout for exceptionally curious people.

Lesson #10: Learn to communicate as clearly as possible to both internal and external audiences.

We shall not cease from exploration

And the end of all our exploring

Will be to arrive where we started

And know the place for the first time.

From 'Little Gidding', T.S. Eliot

CHAPTER 5

Do We Ever Arrive?
Ana's reflections

Change is a constant

That life itself is change was part of the discussions Heraclitus[1] had with his Greek pals as far back as 2500 years ago. The literature of psychotherapy has many accounts showcasing the saga of change, recovery and well-being. The father of modern psychoanalysis, Sigmund Freud, was among the pioneers in publishing research tracking a patient's journey of change. The coaching industry, albeit a younger profession, has likewise produced some brilliant client case studies over the years.[2]

We did not set out to write this book to describe an unusual change journey. Instead, our aim is to bring nuance and transparency, as radical as we can bear, to the otherwise unseen process underpinning the often neatly presented outcome of change in the world of leadership coaching. In other words, rather than prioritizing the coordinates of the destination, ours is an attempt to draw a map of the journey itself.

Saurabh's development is remarkable, unique and a priority for him (and me). There is, however, nothing miraculous about it. Today, it is more common than not for leaders to partner with a coach to become the best version of themselves. Some of these engagements show stronger results than others. That said, as this chapter closely zooms in on Saurabh's change journey, we hope to offer a few additional thoughts, contextualizing the observations made in the previous chapters. If you imagine a map, you may think of these thoughts as topographic lines affording the reader a richer view of the nature of the journey.

In early 2018, at the end of our initial engagement, we assessed Saurabh's development progress following our work over the course of the previous six months. Four years later, Saurabh's development as a leader and as a person has continued. It is impossible to accurately assess what part of the 'Saurabh of today' can directly be attributed to the work we had done years ago. There is a multitude of influences that shapes our life as we go (and grow) through the years.

Quantifying the delta from point A to point B is further complicated by the subjectivity of our assessment of the degree of change that has taken place. As the coach, how biased am I by my vested interest in positive signs of change in my client? After all, is not client progress a reflection of my ability to deliver impact, a stamp of validation for me as a professional?

And Saurabh, who has invested significant emotional energy, mind-space and time into a challenging change process . . . would he not want to record at least a positive trend, if not a positive outcome? We risk falling prey to confirmation bias, a human tendency to process information by searching for and interpreting information that aligns with one's existing beliefs and hopes. And while this bias is often unintentional and unconscious, it can lead to us overlooking or even avoiding information that points in the opposite direction.[3]

These thoughts aside, Saurabh and I both believe there has been a positive change because of our working together. There have been developmental, transitional and transformative types of changes. Saurabh can point to concrete *developmental changes* in the form of added new skills, such as listening more carefully or asking open-ended questions. Saurabh has also replaced his command-and-control leadership style with a more empowering one. As part of this *transitional change*, Saurabh has left the world of corporate employment and embarked on the path of entrepreneurship. In both developmental and transitional modes of change, a leader modifies how he or she behaves and interacts with the world.

In the third mode of change, *transformative change,* we see a leader lean into the unknown and accept the invitation to let go of parts of the old self. Often, this involves exploration of our emotional past and shedding the belief that our temperament is our destiny. It takes great courage to welcome inquiry and to grow in awareness on this frequently uncomfortable path of self-discovery. Saurabh stepped into this challenge, for the first time, five years ago. As a result, Saurabh has adopted a different template of responses to triggers, some of which connect to his formative years. As I look at the Saurabh of today, I see a leader who stands close to his passion and continues to build his authentic presence.

Transformation snapshot

As discussed earlier in the book, in 2017 I had asked Saurabh to take the values-in-action (VIA) assessment of character strengths. This tool, which is part of every engagement I lead, provides a top-down ranking of twenty-four strengths that derive from fundamental traits of human beings. The results showcase which set of strengths makes a client feel energized and experience quick learning curves.[4] At the time, Saurabh's signature strengths were Love of Learning, Creativity, Judgement, Bravery, Appreciation of Beauty and Excellence, in that order. In many ways, this offered an accurate characterization of the Saurabh of that time—keen to master new skills and knowledge, ready to think of novel ways in which to approach his work, careful to evaluate different options, unafraid of adversity and appreciative of top-notch performance.

Exhibit 7: Saurabh's 2017 and 2021 VIA Strengths Profile

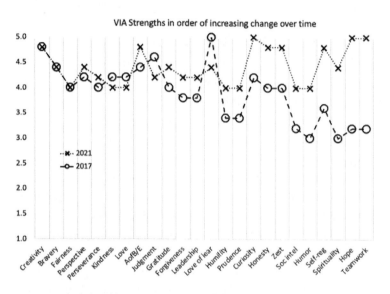

Note regarding the abbreviations used: AofB/E: Appreciation of Beauty and Excellence; Self-reg: Self-Regulation; Love of learn: Love of Learning; Soc intel: Social Intelligence. The full list of the twenty-four strengths can be found here: https://www.viacharacter.org/character-strengths.

Source: viacharacter.org

Fast-forward to December 2021, and Saurabh retook the VIA. The results were in stark contrast to his previous ones. His top strengths now came out as Hope, Curiosity, Teamwork,

Honesty and Creativity, in that order. Creativity was the only strength left from his 2017 top five—only, it had moved from second to fifth place. Taking a first quick glance at Exhibit 7, what stands out are the huge 'jumps' between 2017 and 2021 when it comes to Hope and Teamwork!

Is it possible for such a significant change to happen in one's strengths profile? The short answer is 'yes'. Research shows that while virtues are distinguishing qualities of a particular person, they are indeed not fixed or grounded in immutable biogenetic characteristics. Different from talents and abilities such as intelligence or perfect hearing, which are more innate and less voluntary, strengths or virtues such as kindness can be supported and influenced by context and opportunity. Coaching can offer a platform that raises awareness in a leader, allowing him to make intentional changes, even leading to transformation.

He says, she says, they say

Saurabh says he has changed. I, as his coach, say he's changed. But our holding this view in isolation seemed incomplete as a conclusion as we were writing this book. Our perception may not reflect the reality. Was the change we experienced also noticed by others? And if not, did this offer us an opportunity to close the gap between how Saurabh was perceived by others and what he was in reality?

Understanding and working with the system surrounding a leader generally helps the coach facilitate change in the desired direction. If the system does not change with the leader, it is very difficult for the leader to achieve lasting, positive change.[5] Unless, of course, the leader changes the system or the context itself, which is what Saurabh did eventually, when he left the bank and founded Marcellus.

Keen to answer these questions, I interviewed several key stakeholders who had been important companions on Saurabh's journey, and who are part of his personal and professional system.[6] Most of those I interviewed had known him for several decades, if not his entire life.

As part of these in-depth interviews, I asked several questions, such as: 'How do you know Saurabh?', 'How would you describe Saurabh's key developmental milestones over the years?', 'What change do you notice, if at all, as you interact with the Saurabh of today compared to the Saurabh of 2017?', or 'What is your biggest wish for Saurabh going forward?'

The top five

The VIA is essentially a self-assessment, and we decided to compare Saurabh's view of himself with the feedback on him from stakeholders. The goal was not to produce a scientific research study. Rather, we were interested in picking up key data points and possibly spotting patterns. This is much like what happens in a typical coaching engagement when we run behavioural interviews with a leader's key stakeholders.

Looking at Saurabh's 2021 VIA strengths results, by far the most drastic change is in his number one current strength, Hope, characterized by the conviction that a good future can be brought forward by an individual possessing this strength.[7] While in 2017, Hope had ranked at twenty among the twenty-four traits for Saurabh, by the end of 2021, Hope ranked first. Individuals with this strength strongly agree with statements such as 'I believe that good will triumph over evil', 'I always look on the bright side', or 'Despite challenges, I always remain hopeful about the future'.[8]

The inherent optimism and future orientation of this strength, at its best, carry significant benefits, not only for the individual leader but also for the team. In our interviews, one of Saurabh's team members recalled a particularly dark chapter for Marcellus in 2020: *'The global COVID pandemic was hitting the world hard, and Marcellus was no exception. From one day to the other, we were all working from our home offices, often in a makeshift space between kids playing at one end and dinner being prepared at the other end. The hours were relentless as the demand for our products kept rising. We were working around the clock, all on Zoom. There was no time for our usual banter or coffee chats. After months and months of this, many of us were experiencing signs of exhaustion and depression. One of the levers that got the team through was Saurabh's unrelenting optimism. His energy was contagious as he envisioned, often with data and facts, a bright future for all of us at Marcellus.'*

Gone seemed to be the days when I first met Saurabh in 2017 and he was known for announcing mostly bearish developments in the financial markets on various media channels. Interestingly, now that he looks at the future with a more bullish lens, Saurabh's fame and popularity have not faded, if anything, they seem to have increased.[9] I wonder whether his rising star is in part due to the phenomenon that happy people thrive better than unhappy people.[10]

Curiosity is Saurabh's second top strength; in contrast to pure academic pursuit, Curiosity manifests itself in everyday activities that contribute to rendering life more interesting. Novelty-seeking can be watching the flight of a falcon, being absorbed by a brand-new series on Netflix or exploring new ideas on how to read the markets.

Through my conversations with stakeholders, and especially family members, it is apparent that Saurabh has been fiercely curious all his life. Curiosity also ranked high in his 2017 report. This strength can offer fuel for a balanced life and can positively contribute to a leader's stress management as it typically helps a leader to be curious also beyond work, exploring various aspects of life. This book is in part likely also a credit to his curiosity.[11] Saurabh's keen wish to understand our 2017 process was what first planted the seeds for this venture.

Teamwork is another one of Saurabh's top five strengths. Here we see another huge jump—in 2017 Teamwork came in at 22/24, but by the end of 2021, it ranked 3/24. Markers of Teamwork include working well as a member of a group, being loyal to the group and being prepared to do one's share. Not surprisingly, Saurabh's deep concern for the Marcellus team emerges regularly when we speak. The idea of collaboration is of great importance to Saurabh. As one of the interviewed stakeholders, who had also worked for Saurabh in the previous company, described it: *'In our leadership meetings today, when there is a disagreement in the team, Saurabh will let others drive the decision-making even if he disagrees with them in about half the cases. Whereas prior to the coaching in 2017, Saurabh would, in 90 per cent of the cases, choose the "my way or the highway" approach.'*

There is also Saurabh's concern for the well-being of the collective, which has expressed itself in his commitment to not push people beyond their limits. *'There are forums where there is no agenda; we may be together as a team and there are moments when we see him smile, crack jokes. That did not happen before 2017.'*

As one looks at Saurabh's trajectory, he, like many senior leaders, started out as an individual contributor before he assumed various leadership roles. Most talent experiences some struggles in this transition, due to a lack of experience and training in how to lead a team. A notable change in Saurabh's leadership philosophy and style has also been described by one of the Marcellus team members who knows Saurabh for two decades: *'While at the bank, Saurabh used to express his frustration with slower or less talented members with regular emotional outbursts, including hitting his fists on the table. Since the coaching intervention, he has grown more accepting of the inefficiencies of the world. He is still leading from the front and will hold people accountable, but in an empowering fashion.'*

What is interesting to note is that while there was regular attrition at the bank, attrition at Marcellus is close to zero. In part, it is because the recruitment process for new team members is carefully designed to select for shared values such as 'team first, individual second'. As one of Saurabh's direct reports explained: *'Our culture is very positive; we are encouraged to do what we want to do, we can grow in our roles and beyond and we have a personal stake in the business.'*

Markers for his number four strength of Honesty are a commitment to be true to oneself and to lead and live authentically. Reflecting on Saurabh's professional trajectory, through founding Marcellus there seems to be a greater alignment between who he is and what he does. As an entrepreneur, he also has greater autonomy—not only to choose what he does but also how he does it. Authenticity is at the core of Honesty, and statements such as 'It is more important to be myself than to be popular', 'I would never lie just to get something I wanted from someone', or 'My life is guided and given meaning by my code of values', are endorsed by individuals who hold this particular strength.

Saurabh is a man of principles. When I spoke with a family member as part of this exercise, it did not surprise me to hear that a strong framework of values and principles was integral to his upbringing. One of the core values in his family of origin is the importance of prioritizing learning: *'We would always encourage Saurabh to choose books over clothes or other gadgets.'* Reinforcing this value, Saurabh's family cherishes its Bengali roots, Bengalis being known for their intellect.[12]

Another family value is about contributing to the greater good. As I have come to understand, for Saurabh, as a leader and an individual, making money is not his primary motivator, despite his tenure and success of over two decades in the finance sector. Rendering Marcellus profitable is a marker of success for him if it stands in support of those that matter to him: his family, his team and his clients.

His honesty also manifests in his candour of speech, which he brings to work. One of the stakeholders commented: '*A lot of brokers are on TV. Saurabh differs as he not only ran some very interesting research but he was also refreshingly honest in his assessments, not a very common quality in the industry.*'

Our values and principles tend to be instilled in us during our formative years. A significant part of any coaching engagement is about bringing awareness to a leader as to his or her own set of existing values and allowing him or her to then make intentional choices as to which values to keep, which to discard and which ones to add to the mix of desirable values.

Creativity, Saurabh's fifth top strength, is known to carry transformational powers. A key marker of Creativity is a drive to think of new and productive ways to approach challenges. And while there may be some artistic talent involved, Creativity manifests in one's approach to processes and problem-solving. Highly creative people tend to agree with statements such as 'I am very independent', 'I am a risk-taker' and 'I am very curious'. Highly creative individuals also tend to have a high IQ.

Without exception, Saurabh has been described by those whom I interviewed as a fiercely independent spirit. One of Saurabh's trademarks is that he thinks outside the box: '*His mind never stops. Where others see roadblocks, he will see opportunities. And it seems that by leading Marcellus, he has created an environment that facilitates creativity in all of us, as we have an open and informal culture.*'

Another marker of creative leaders is their proclivity to work on several projects simultaneously, often generating ideas for one project while still working on another, cross-fertilization of ideas being a positive by-product. Writing books seems to be for Saurabh a way to capture as well as generate ideas.

Our Achilles heel lies in our strengths

The impact of our strengths correlates with how well we understand how to use them. And, contrary to what one might think, it is not in the lowest-ranking strengths where our derailers hide. It is often in the under- or overuse of our top strengths that our greatest vulnerabilities can be found. It is here that we fall short of our potential, where life energy gets wasted and where we cause the most suffering, for ourselves and for others.

Exhibit 8: Saurabh's top strengths and their optimal use

Strength	Underuse	Optimal Use	Overuse
Hope	Negative; Past-oriented	Positive expectations; Optimistic	Unrealistic; Blind optimism
Curiosity	Bored; Apathetic	Intrigued; Open	Nosy; Intrusive
Teamwork	Self-serving; Individualistic	Loyal; Collaborative	Dependent; Loss of individuality
Honesty	Phony; Inauthentic	True to oneself; Sincere	Self-righteous; Rude
Creativity	Conforming; Plain	Uniqueness that is practical; Original	Eccentric; Odd

Source: www.viacharacter.org

Reviewing Saurabh's risk profile and our discussions, I wonder whether *overuse of Hope* may make him on occasion less perceptive during times when others need him to slow down and acknowledge their concerns. How did he see this play out during the pandemic? Might an *overuse of Honesty* risk Saurabh coming off as disrespectful? And, as Saurabh is more of an introvert, might he sometimes stay too much in his own head and *underuse Curiosity* vis-à-vis those around him?

We often look for strengths to complement each other and to keep the spikes that come from under- or overuse of them 'in check'. Frequently, I encourage leaders to look at their 'middle strengths' (rank 8–16 out of the total of 24 strengths) to find such support. For example, in Saurabh's 2021 Strength Profile, Teamwork is his third highest strength. If overdone, he might shy away from having difficult conversations. Here his middle strength of Bravery, ranked 12, could help him as the leader to challenge the team when they are being too cautious.

A shift from knowing to finding meaning

Most of Saurabh's top-tier strengths in 2017 came under the virtues of *Cognitive Strengths*. Some of them were Love of Learning, Creativity, Judgement and Curiosity. As we review his 2021 results, we can see the aspect of *Transcendence Strengths*[13] take on a greater presence through Hope, Appreciation of Beauty and Excellence, and Spirituality. Transcendence-group strengths are those that help one forge connections beyond the self. You might say they lift our gaze from the map of the terrain beneath us to the chart of the stars above. Here a leader experiences significant energy around the themes of purpose and meaning. Creating a legacy, giving back, uplifting not only self but also others, are central themes in this space.

And the biggest wish (of others) is for Saurabh to . . .

If you google Saurabh Mukherjea, the list of achievements and accolades that comes up seems endless. After a successful career in corporate India, Saurabh has launched his own firm, which he has strongly led through a health pandemic and global economic volatility. A bestselling author of six books, Saurabh regularly appears in the media and is seen on worldwide panels and speaker circuits. In his personal life, he has been happily married to his childhood sweetheart for twenty-three years, and they have two teenage children who are thriving.

Saurabh seems to have it all. And it is this very sentence which, whenever I hear it, makes me wonder whether there is a hidden wish that people have for him. When I asked stakeholders what their wish for Saurabh is, their vote was unanimous: it was for Saurabh to slow down. More specifically, they wished for him to 'chill', 'smell the roses', 'manage his stress', 'take his foot off the gas', 'enjoy his success' and just 'be'.

Saurabh seems to have been born with more life energy than most of us. One of my favourite moments during the interviews was when I asked stakeholders to complete the following sentence: 'When I think of Saurabh at age ten, I see . . .'

Here are some excerpts from their responses:

'I see a perpetually active boy, reading a lot, taking a lot in. And I see him being talkative about what he just learnt, running around, always doing something, eyes wide open.'

'I see him as sporty, a big fan of cricket, and knowing more about it than any of his friends.'

'I see infinite energy, packed into a tiny human. There is a sparkle in his eye and a hint of mischief, but a heart of gold. This boy is full of adventure, ready to make his mark in the world.'

'I see a boy with big brown eyes, and even when he had to sit still, legs were still swinging in a carefree manner.'

'I see him as always being outside, riding his bicycle all day. A wide grin on his face, he would rub the dirt off his clothes as his mother scolded him for being home late again. Only for this to repeat the next day.'

'I see him with a dishevelled head full of brown curls, bright-eyed, out for the next adventure, never standing still.'

'Intelligent, he was often lost in his own thoughts. When he would come home from school, only in shorts and T-shirt, the school uniform forgotten back in class.'

Exhibit 9:

WordArt-based responses by stakeholders on the question: When I think of Saurabh at age ten

Telling a man brimming with energy to sit down comes close to torture for him. Coaches need to remain nuanced in their effort to support clients. Stress itself is neither good nor bad.[14] It comes down to regulating the amount of stress a leader experiences and finding that happy medium where productivity is high that the leader and the team are in 'flow', and everyone can stay clear of burnout. In other words, as long as we actively manage stress, we can stay in that healthy-stress zone.

Exhibit 10: The Yerkes Dodson Law: How Anxiety affects Performance[15]

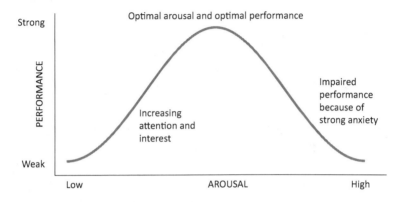

Source: Harvard Business Review

Saurabh is in a state of 'flow' when he does research on the markets, when he reads a book in his leisure time on a subject that he finds interesting. His nightstand always has at least five books on it that he is reading simultaneously. An introvert at heart, he gets joy out of deeply connecting with one or two people at a time.

This is very different from 'bad stress', where pressures mount so high that performance and well-being suffer. This is where Saurabh used to spend most of his time when we first met. He has since learnt to seek a relaxation response, to step away from the trigger and only to come back once the nervous system has had a chance to calm down. It is here where he steps back into the creative zone that he can lead successfully.

Hearing what his stakeholders have to say about him, I wonder if he is doing this enough. What makes them concerned for him? What might we have to look at together to ensure he actively manages his energy reserves? Having founded a company and having led it through a pandemic is no easy charge. In today's world of complexity and its many challenges, including war, it is even more critical for leaders to assume responsibility for consistently monitoring and managing their stress.

Going back to the root cause of the problem is key for forward change to stick

Another way to gauge where we must direct our agenda for change is to look for markers of emotional well-being. Self-acceptance, vulnerability towards self, trust in others as well as an ability to communicate so we can assert our needs and wants, and by the same token, inspiring those around us, are all important markers. The less we have been knocked in our formative years, the stronger we tend to emerge on these markers. Contrary to what some argue, a leader's childhood does matter.[16]

Most of us, even if we grew up in a loving childhood home with caring parental figures, will have experienced some form of psychological bruising—an adored parent who is one day hot and the next day cold, a divorce and sense of balance lost, a bully in middle school who torments our every day.

I remember working with Jim, a leader at an FTSE-500 company, who would regularly, when faced with interpersonal confrontation, withdraw. It was as if someone had flipped a switch; his attention would drift off, and even if he was still physically in the room, it seemed to others that he was no longer 'there'. Jim was on autopilot; his past was driving his present actions. And despite his acute awareness of the problem, his desire to change and his access to 'tools' to do so, he felt stuck. It was only once we explored the unique history of his childhood that he was able to get unstuck. It turns out that when Jim was growing up, his father, once back from work, often would 'withdraw' from him at the family home. After countless vain attempts to get his father's attention, withdrawal seemed a perfectly normal response, and Jim had been applying the 'withdrawal strategy' to his relationships as an adult too.[17]

Once a leader understands the connection between his or her past and present, the opportunity to break its spell emerges. As does the opportunity to get off autopilot and intentionally embrace some of the key messages of the connection that still resonate with us today.

Saurabh's reflections

On roots

As Ana highlights in the next chapter of this book, a big part of my life plays out inside my mind. By nature, I am an introvert and, as the comment from one of my closest relatives in this chapter reveals, from my childhood days, I have had the ability to stay inside my mind for hours on end, utterly oblivious to what is happening in the world around me. As I grew older, this ability to zone in helped me excel, first in academics and then in the stock market. My ability to absorb lots of information, turn it into a mental model, play with that model in my head for hours on end and thus see the world in ways no one else can has been a great asset for me professionally.

However, when it comes to building close relationships with friends, with my family and with other people that I love, the same trait becomes a handicap. Since I stay in my mind so much, many people perceive me to be distant, aloof and uncaring. For example, in the middle of a social gathering, I might be focusing on understanding how many or how few people are using ride-sharing rather than their own cars to arrive at the social gathering. For the most part, I did not care so much about this aspect of my life—other people and how I interacted with them and what they made of me—until I met Ana in 2017 courtesy of my erstwhile employer.

As I read the VIA Pro feedback contained in this chapter and the comments from the people who have known me for most of my life, my mind went back to 2017, the year in which Ana and I started working together.

As described in Chapter 3, in autumn 2017, Ana had given me some of the most difficult-to-digest feedback that I have received in my life. The feedback came from my closest colleagues in my previous firm. It also came from other board directors with whom I had attended dozens of board meetings over the years and whose opinion was taken seriously in the Indian business community. While that feedback had stung, it had also made me determined to do something about it because—to my mind—the person that my erstwhile colleagues were describing in 2017 did not feel like the real me. While I still don't fully understand what my true personality is, the feedback contained in this chapter feels closer to the person I truly am—a hard-working, driven, sincere individual trying to do the best he can for his family, his colleagues, his friends and his clients. You could say that the hard yards that Ana and I have put in over the past several years have culminated in the feedback contained in this chapter. To that extent, the feedback in this chapter—both Ana's and the people she spoke to—feels like a milestone in my personal development.

However, as I read Ana's feedback contained in this chapter, something even more interesting has happened. As I see myself described by the people I love and whose opinions I value, I realize that both in my strengths and in my weaknesses, in my achievements and in my failures, I am a reflection of my parents and—even more interestingly—my grandparents. I guess, like many other people, I am so convinced that I am making my own way through the world that the realization of my ancestors' fingerprints being all over me hadn't hit home—until today.

Once I started seeing myself through the prism of my parents and grandparents' personalities, a lot of things fell into place, and many decisions that I have taken over the course of my life started making sense.

All four of my grandparents were highly articulate, super-active people. Both my grandfathers were successful lawyers in Kolkata, and right through my childhood and teenage years I grew accustomed to seeing long queues of clients waiting patiently outside their offices. My paternal grandmother was a social worker of repute, a voracious reader and the life and soul of our ancestral home in Kolkata, where I would spend most of my summer holidays. My maternal grandmother was a domineering woman who ran her household with an iron fist, and she had strong opinions about most people and most topics under the sun.

My grandparents used to visit us every year in Delhi, and I used to visit Kolkata every year to spend my six-week summer holiday with them. Spending so much time with them meant that I was deeply influenced not just by the love they showered upon my sister and me but also by their life experiences, their ability to be a force for change in society, their hunger for reading, their love of travelling, their obsession with good food and their love of life in general. Looking back at their lives ten to twenty years after they have passed away, I can see now how my grandparents influenced my parents and how many of those influences rubbed off on me. For example, long before

I became an adult, it was a no-brainer for me that a house worth living in is a house stuffed full of good books. Spending the entire weekend reading, thinking and conversing about politics, sports, music and the arts was how I thought everyone lived, until I grew up and realized that there are such things as partying, nightlife, drinking and dancing.

However, just as my grandparents' positive influences rubbed off on my parents and on myself, their negatives also played a role in our lives. For example, both my grandfathers had volcanic tempers. While neither of them was physically imposing, decades of arguing matters in court had given them strong voices, and when they lost their temper and shouted, I saw as a child that everyone else around them trembled.

On my father's side, I don't think my paternal grandparents ever fully got over the fact that the Partition of India in 1947 meant that they lost everything they had (which they had to leave behind in what was first called East Pakistan and subsequently became Bangladesh). And while my paternal grandparents successfully rebuilt their lives in Kolkata, the loss of their ancestral property, of their livelihood and of friendships, was something that gnawed away at them even half a century later.

Then, when I was eight years old, my paternal grandparents lost one of their sons—one of my father's two brothers died of pneumonia in his mid-forties. He was a talented man—an engineering graduate from India's premier engineering college (IIT Mumbai), the secretary of his college student union and subsequently an entrepreneur blessed with brains and good looks. I still remember my grandmother weeping for days on end as she mourned her son, my uncle.

Losing their home to Partition and then losing a son left scars on my paternal grandparents, and it made them introspective and melancholic in the final decades of their lives. I was a teenager by the time my grandparents reached the twilight of their lives, and I tried my level best to spend as much time as I could with them, even though by then we lived in London and they in Kolkata.

I saved up money from working—first in a bathroom fittings store and then in a betting shop—to fund my trips to Kolkata. As I sat with my paternal grandparents on their balcony on balmy evenings in Kolkata, with the stars twinkling and a gentle breeze rustling the bougainvillea plants (which still adorn the balcony of my ancestral home), I absorbed some of their introspective and melancholic nature.

With the benefit of hindsight, I can now see that as I learnt to see the world through their eyes, I had realized as a teenager that much of what we tend to get excited about when we are young—wealth, power, friends, community, respect—is transient. By this time, we had been through several difficult years in the UK and, thanks to my grandparents' reminiscing about their lives, by my teenage years I had built a mental model that in life, I too would learn to take the smooth with the rough. In fact, it was in those years that I instinctively memorized the lyrics of the Dire Straits song, 'The Bug' (1992):[18]

Sometimes you're the windshield
Sometimes you're the bug
Sometimes it all comes together baby
Sometimes you're a fool in love
Sometimes you're the Louisville slugger
Sometimes you're the ball
Sometimes it all comes together baby
Sometimes you're going to lose it all

Even today, I hum these words to myself, both on days when I am feeling on top of the world and on days when I feel miserable. And to this day, I try to ensure that at least once every six months, I go back to my paternal grandparents' house in Kolkata and sit on the balcony and listen to the breeze rustling the bougainvillea plants. That's enough to bring back the bittersweet memories of my moonlit chats with them.

When my paternal grandmother died in a car crash in northern India in 1999, she was seventy-five years old. It took me a few years to process what had happened. I remember I was working as an economist in London at that time. When my mother called on a weekday afternoon at 3 p.m. to convey the news that my grandmother was dead, I passed out even before I could put the phone down. My colleagues were kind enough to help me recover, put me in a taxi and send me home. Thankfully, Sarbani was staying with me then and she used to take me on long walks to help me talk about my grandmother and how much I missed her.

A quarter of a century on from my paternal grandmother Shephalika Mukherjea's demise, I still think about her every day. In 2016, I dedicated my first bestseller, *The Unusual Billionaires*, to her. She loved me unconditionally, as I suppose grandmothers the world over do. By the time I entered my teens, she realized that, with my introversion and my upbringing, I would amount to something. In the years before she died, she ensured that I understood that I had the talent and the capability to make something of my life. From the time I was six, she would take me to her social-work meetings in orphanages and schools in Kolkata. While travelling to these meetings, she would tell me that all of us had to stand up and make a difference if we were to deal with the grinding poverty that continues to characterize many parts of India. My father, too, absorbed these influences from his mother, and throughout my teenage years, it was drummed into my head that 'a life just spent in earning lots of money is a life wasted'.

My parents not only suffered all of the reverses mentioned above even more keenly than I did, but they also had an additional burden to deal with—from the 1960s to the 1980s, many Indian leaders across the political spectrum fell prey to a specific brand of socialism, which ran the economy to the ground and destroyed the hopes of a whole generation of bright, hardworking Indians, including my parents. As a result, my abiding memory of my childhood years is of my parents discussing on a weekly basis how little money we had and how little we could do to improve our standard of living.

My grandparents' lives had moments of great joy interspersed with the loss of loved ones and the loss of livelihood. Their strengths and their preferences seeped into me and made me what I am. Their traumas and their yearning for a better life (or perhaps for a better world) gave me my workaholism and my determination to succeed. Having seen good people, hard-working, decent, honest people get a raw deal from a very early age, I want to redress the imbalance.

Everything I do is my way of ensuring that the next generation of Indians—my children's generation—does not have to get the raw deal that my parents and my grandparents did. As I explain in the final chapter of the book, there is plenty left for me to do—for my family, for Marcellus and for India. I see every day as an opportunity to make a difference to all three of these constituencies, and that is why I won't stop running as hard as I can.

What I have learnt from Ana is to take whatever I have— my roots, my memories, my upbringing, my value systems and my abilities—and channel them constructively so that rather than damaging myself (through overwork, through self-neglect) and my relationships with other people (by steamrolling over them), I find my way in the world with a sense of balance. I now try to balance what I want to achieve with what people around me would like to achieve. I try to balance the needs of my body and my family's needs with my professional goals. Another way of putting this is: I try to balance the future (and the zillion different things I would like to do) with the present. I try to live outside my mind more than I used to. As you will read in the next chapter, Ana has found clever ways to coax me to live outside my mind a little bit more than I would have, left to my own devices!

Ana's reflections

One step at a time

I am grateful to Saurabh for taking me on this journey back to his roots. As we work with leaders, these glimpses into someone's upbringing are invaluable. Let me just add that, of course, that is not the end all and be all. The past does explain some of our present way of being. In fact, while being aware of one's past is important, we must also keep in mind that our past is not our destiny. With all my clients—and this is a core premise of coaching—I advocate the element of freedom of choice. Rather than being prisoner to our emotions, we have a choice as to how we see our lives and how we act in our lives. Austrian psychiatrist Alfred Adler, a giant in the field of psychology and one of the travel companions of Freud, promoted the notion that we are not determined by our past and what we experience but rather by what meaning we assign to them: '*The important thing is not what one is born with, but what use one makes of this equipment.*' And while Adler as an individual scholar is long forgotten by most, his research has influenced a slew of great business literature, including Steven Covey's classic leadership read, *The 7 Habits of Highly Effective People.*[19]

Saurabh has chosen to make changes, big and small. And it does give me a sense of joy when I see tangible evidence emerge in unexpected places. Yesterday, I wrote Saurabh a note while he was on vacation. What a surprise when I received this automatic reply: 'I am on leave and won't be checking my emails. For urgent requests, please contact my office at . . .' This is the first time since I've known Saurabh that he has set a boundary so clearly. There it is: positive, continuous change. One step at a time.

Key Takeaways

- Very few coaching engagements gauge change over time. We measured change over a five-year time horizon. There has been developmental (new skills added), transitional (moved to empowering leadership from command-and-control), and transformative (different responses to triggers) change as a result of our working together.
- A leader's childhood matters when it comes to achieving transformative change. Once a leader understands the connection between past and present, the opportunity to break its spell emerges—as does the opportunity to get off autopilot and to make better, intentional choices.
- Strengths may change over time and it is useful to re-assess them every so often. A comparison of a strengths assessment from 2017 to 2021 shows a significant jump in some strengths, such as Hope and Teamwork for Saurabh. It is a powerful illustration of transformative change.
- Change assessed in isolation is meaningless. Perception is reality. Coaches also need to assess how the system around a client perceives that change: has it in fact taken place and to what degree?
- Stress itself is neither good nor bad. It comes down to regulating the amount and type of stress a leader experiences and finding that happy medium where productivity is high and where the leader and the team can experience a state of 'flow' and well-being.

There are many here among us

Who feel that life is but a joke

But you and I, we've been through that

And this is not our fate

So let us stop talkin' falsely now

The hour's getting late.

'All Along the Watchtower' (1967), Bob Dylan

CHAPTER **6**

In Session: A Coaching Conversation
Ana's reflections

It's a first

I witnessed my first 'fishbowl'[1] at the Harvard Medical School coaching conference in 2009, where I, as a founding fellow of the Harvard Institute of Coaching, was privileged to witness 'what happens live' during a coaching session. The coach, who was also the head coach at Google at the time, and the client, an executive from the Boston area, were sitting on a raised stage in front of a group of coaches and business leaders. One could have heard a needle drop to the floor; it was so quiet in the room. The opportunity to eavesdrop on what usually is a strictly confidential conversation rarely comes along.

Yet, listening in and observing others is how we can learn—or at least this is what allows us to get a sense of potential approaches to a client challenge. There may be thought-provoking or non-intuitive angles a coach takes that we can integrate into our own practice or, equally, gain clarity on what *not* to do. This is the reason why Saurabh and I ultimately decided to publish an account of a real dialogue between the two of us. What you will read in this chapter is an excerpt from several conversations on a current challenge Saurabh is facing as he continues to lead Marcellus.

You will see us zeroing in on how to effectively have difficult conversations and influence in a way that is constructive and supports not only the team and the business but also its clients. This area was also part of our initial work in 2017, when Saurabh's challenge had been to become a more empowering leader, capable of building bridges with others and in the most difficult of circumstances.

It is not surprising that there was still fresh ground for Saurabh to cover in this important territory. As I look at my current client portfolio, there is an even greater demand for learning how to lead a team in these complex and challenging post-pandemic times. The resilience of many leaders and their people has worn thin, and we do know that in the face of great pressure, our derailers surface more readily than during good times.

What you will read here are verbatim excerpts from our discussions as coach and client.[2] This chapter also captures our reflections and thoughts about the conversation, how we think it went, what we believe was useful and what was less useful, and the insights or further questions that may have surfaced as a result of these conversations.

One general observation is about the importance of silence. The excerpts we've curated are obviously chosen to allow insight into the process, but it might be worth noting that, sometimes, pauses (even uncomfortably long ones) are key to allowing a client to fully explore what is happening. They were therefore an integral part of the coaching, even though they are not specifically pointed out in the following excerpts.

Finally, these are excerpts of our coaching conversations, not complete transcripts of our coaching sessions. To avoid too lengthy a read, we selected those parts that we hope are of interest to the reader.

Fishbowl Conversation, Excerpts

Excerpt 1, May 2022 via Zoom

Ana: A warm welcome to our coaching session, Saurabh. As you and I had agreed, this session is being recorded and transcribed . . . are you still comfortable with that?

(**A's reflections**: In these sessions, there is the audible conversation in the room, between Saurabh and me, and then there is the silent conversation that I am having with myself. Such parallel processing encompasses the client, me and the dynamic in the room—during and post sessions. Noticing these different elements allows me to better separate what is my material versus the client's. Equally, useful information for future sessions often emerges.

In this context of recording our sessions, knowing that our conversation will be made public as one of the chapters in this book, I notice that there is a part of me that feels more self-conscious than usual. Will I be able to focus fully on the coaching conversation? What will other professionals think as they read this? Might they not judge me? I understand that despite being a seasoned coach, at this point I am fallible and will make the wrong moves and miss opportunities. But then again, I have learnt that my fallibility has yielded important learning opportunities and often moves the needle for the client and their challenge.

Still, I tell myself that a heightened self-consciousness may interfere with my ability to be present in the conversation. It is key that I stay focused.)

Saurabh: Hi Ana, yes, that is fine by me.

(**S's reflections**: I surprise myself by being fine with recording a real-life coaching session. A part of me is, of course, a bit wary. How will others perceive this? How might their view of me change as a result of reading this? At the same time, I feel like the whole power of this book lies in this very chapter. This is where we let the reader peek behind the curtain of a real coaching session. This is where what is usually confidential becomes public. There is also a part of me that wonders whether some of the subtleties of this conversation will translate well in written form. The reader will see excerpts, not the full session. They will not know when there are pauses, when I receive a supportive smile or a nod from Ana that diffuses some of the challenge that some of her questions bring. Regardless of all these limitations of the printed word, I am convinced that readers will benefit immensely from this chapter, not least because it will help them gain more clarity on what happens behind the scenes. Perhaps one of the reasons I asked Ana to co-write this book was to get to know her better as a person and therefore understand how she has been able to help me. As I write down these reflections, I also wonder why I have this need to crack the 'Da Vinci Code' on our coaching's success.)

A: Great. Saurabh, you had mentioned in our discussions that you wanted to explore the area of conflict some more. What specifically would you like to talk about here?

(**A's reflections**: This is an important topic for many of my clients. It is also one that I've personally had to work on, given my own story. When I was growing up, conflict in my family quickly got hot and loud, only to cool off the next moment and then be forgotten the following day. There was no exploration of what had gone wrong or how to approach difficult situations better next time. I entered adulthood struggling with the idea of conflict, and it was only my training as a mediator and as a coach and therapist that allowed me to see conflict for what it is at its finest: a driver for better understanding of others, an opportunity to grow and develop as an individual, and an invitation to strengthen our connection with those around us. In business, it is rarely the team of like-minded equals that brims with creativity; it is the team that acknowledges, explores and exploits its differences, and as a result, drives innovation, that does.

And yet, conflict remains a complex topic for me. In my personal life, I occasionally find myself being triggered by some things others say, and it takes me constant reminders to separate what is taking place right in front of me from what is a ghost from the past that comes into the room and risks derailing my reactions. If staying in an adult voice is hard and sometimes impossible for a trained professional, how much harder must it be for clients! Working with a client in this complex area requires the coach to often tread lightly, to remain patient. And for sustainable progress to take place, it is important to explore the past and the present with a client, cognizant that this is not therapy despite my using some therapeutic interventions.)

S: Hmmmm . . . because of our work together five years ago, I have learnt to face tension and obstacles without getting emotionally hijacked. Today, I rarely aggress the other party in the form of cutting them off or shouting at them. This works quite well when I like someone or am at least neutral towards the other. What also helps me is that I have learnt to manage my stress levels better and therefore I get less triggered. However, I feel a little lost when I do not like my counterpart. Then my more aggressive self threatens to make an appearance.

(A's reflections: I make a note to come back to the idea of 'liking'; what makes Saurabh like or dislike someone? What makes them neutral for him? What makes it harder to contain himself when he dislikes someone?)

A: It sounds like you feel stuck when it comes to how to solve these interpersonal challenges and tensions when you do not feel connected to the other person. And I can imagine that it can be frustrating on a personal level and possibly nerve-racking on a professional one. What are you hoping for and what do you need to get from today's conversation?

S: I really need to learn how to have difficult conversations in any situation and with anyone. That is important for me in my role at Marcellus. I know that aggressing the other is not the answer, so how do I approach difficult discussions with people I don't like?

(S's reflections: A way to avoid conflict would be to run a small business, one that offers me and my colleagues a comfortable life. And if Marcellus is a small business in a large market like India, I can limit myself to dealing only with people that I like. But my colleagues and I are also ambitious about Marcellus and don't want it to be a small, boutique operation. That, in turn, means I must go out there and meet people I don't necessarily like. This is one of the tensions I must resolve as Marcellus continues to scale up.)

A: Yes, the 'how to' of having constructive conflict is important both personally and when running a business. The groundwork for this is often laid in our earlier life experiences. The 'why' is also an important question to answer when we struggle with asserting our needs effectively. Would you want to explore together what conflict was like when you were growing up?

(A's reflections: As we discuss his personal experience with conflict in the context of his family of origin, I notice Saurabh's face occasionally becomes tight, his eyes briefly close and a pained expression flashes across his face. It is as if he does not want to 'face it'—an avoidance that manifests itself physically. There is in Saurabh's story, as for many families, some struggle when it comes to having difficult conversations in a constructive manner. I find myself admiring Saurabh's courage and am grateful for his openness and trust, as this is where the work begins. Going to the source of one's world view and behaviour in the here and now is important for a leader to begin to move away from autopilot and to make intentional choices from his new-found awareness. Saurabh and I have discussed his past numerous times before, and in this session, we go a bit further in detail. And as part of our work together, by 2022, he has modified and moved away from the conflict model he had known growing up.[3] Building on Saurabh's story, I lead us back into the here and now with an observation.)

A: There seems to be a significant difference in how you experience conflict when it comes to people that you like or are neutral towards versus people that you dislike. Can you share a bit more here?

S: I like most people or am neutral towards them. People that I have a natural dislike for are those who have a big ego, are very commercial and seem to think mostly about their own benefits. Sometimes that can go as far as them engaging in ethically questionable behaviour.

(**A's reflections**: I am making a note to explore this further at a later point in time. Saurabh is running a business, and so, while I can relate to unethical behaviour, such as bribery, being unacceptable, I am surprised by his reacting so strongly to people in the financial services industry being commercial. Also, what is it about a 'big ego'—what does it constitute for him, and where is his own ego in all of this? Might there be a potential insecurity that stems from running a boutique firm and facing off against giant financial services institutions?

Often, a strong reaction towards someone can be also a form of projection. Seeing a quality we dislike manifest in someone else is as if they are holding up a mirror to us and to what we reject in ourselves. And through attacking them, we attack that part we dislike in ourselves. It is a well-researched phenomenon described by the British-Austrian psychoanalyst Melanie Klein. In Saurabh's case, I was wondering, is there a part of him that likes being in the spotlight, that enjoys attention? And is that possibly a reaction that has its roots in the lack of attention he received when he first moved to the UK as an adolescent?)

A: Can you give me an example of a difficult conversation that went well for you with someone that you like or are neutral towards?

S: Yes. A couple of years ago, one of my team members wanted to be paid more and we sat down together. I walked him through the logic of how this would not be possible in the short term, but how he would catch up in the longer run. Alternatively, we also talked about how he could be paid faster and how that would need to involve a role change. I knew I could not give him exactly what he wanted, but by helping him see the logic and options, we came to a good outcome. I guess one thing that helps me have these difficult conversations is not only liking the person but also preparing for these moments and carefully thinking through what I am going to say.

(**A's reflections:** It seems there is an element of wanting to keep control here. The idea of not liking other Alphas . . . does he also dislike the idea that they might intellectually be at par or even 'out-think' him, and so there's a risk that he might lose control over the process? An Alpha himself, much of his source of influence and power has come from leading with his intellect and ingenuity, starting in his teenage years. I also wonder, how does his tendency to favour intellect over emotion impact his relationships?)

A: In these instances when you feel like the challenging conversation goes well, you come prepared, you make sure you have sufficient time in hand. You also shared that it helps you to like the person. How much is this sentiment of 'liking' connected to how well you know them?

(**A's reflections**: It may feel repetitive for me to paraphrase the client's statement. Yet, this is an important element in any coaching dialogue as it lets the coach be sure he or she heard the client right, make course corrections, helps build client rapport and role-models one element of listening skills that clients can integrate into their own practice.)

S: Hmmm . . . interesting.

(**S's reflections**: True—it often feels like I know the people I like quite well, or at least that I understand what their core values are. In fact, thanks to Ana's coaching, over the past few years I have learnt to invest considerable time and effort in getting to know better the people that I like.)

A: Even people we know can and will surprise us with their reactions. I am wondering how curious [you are] to allow yourself to get in those conversations and explore what the other person needs and wants. In short, how much do you ask versus tell?

S: Now that you say it, I realize I need to ask more questions . . . I remember the article well that you had sent me a while back. I think it was an HBR article titled 'The Business Case for Curiosity'.[4]

A: Asking more questions sounds like a great idea, as it plays to one of your signature strengths, Curiosity. Why do you think you are not using it more, currently?

(**A's reflections**: You will notice that I again gently reminded Saurabh of his strengths; in particular Curiosity, as he is clearly underusing it, even as he approaches conversations with people he likes. We know that energy and excellence result from using our strengths, and I make sure to integrate this into my coaching wherever possible.)

S: Not sure . . .

A: Listening to you, I feel like there may be a wish to get difficult conversations done and over with. This can be a form of avoidance . . . what might you be wanting to avoid?

S: True. I am keen for there to be a positive outcome and a way forward.

A: Is that all? Most of us enjoy ticking off boxes on tasks at hand; is there a bit of that in there as well? Do you think you sacrifice exploration as you seek to be efficient?

S: (laughs) Yes, bang on. I am working on that; I must manage the balance between efficiency and effectiveness, which is not always the same.

(**S's reflections**: In the past, when Marcellus was small, I was personally involved in every part of the business. Now, given that the firm has grown much bigger, I have tried to delegate as much as possible, not only to empower the other leaders in the firm but also to manage my time and my stress levels so I can be the best version of a leader for them.)

A: I wonder whether there is an avoidance element here as well, as you seem to want to move away from difficult dialogues not only as you face an uncomfortable party but also when you deal with what you call a likeable or neutral counterpart. I am spotting a pattern here, what do you think?

(A's reflections: Avoidance is a central theme. If we second-guess what someone wants from us, or how we might solve someone's challenge, we are not allowing any real authentic relationship to develop between us. The other party is in a relationship with our fantasy of what we think the other party needs. Figuratively speaking, we put up a screen, and the other is in relationship with what we project. Psychologically speaking, it is a defence against a real interaction that might hurt us or compromise our desire for control. So, instead of an interaction, we are seeing a transaction. Authentic closeness is tough, but this is where the connection happens and that is when we can lead from the heart.)

S: Yes, there might be something to this, this avoidance bit.

(S's reflections: I can feel the questions are becoming deeper and tougher. Ana takes my mind to places I don't naturally gravitate towards. In fact, one of the reasons I have benefited from Ana's coaching is that she compels me to go down mental pathways that I am, if left to my own devices, reluctant to explore. Coaching sessions with Ana force me to confront the weaknesses in my mental make-up. As Ana and I are having this discussion, I realize that it is getting late in the day here in Mumbai and I just want to pull the shutters down and wind up for the day. And yet, what keeps me motivated is that I trust Ana and she has shown me again and again that she has my best interests at heart. Given that I want to grow, I want to develop as a person and leader, learning from these coaching sessions with Ana is important for me no matter how late in the day it is in Mumbai. This part of me wins on the occasion. In fact, this part of me wins most of the time.)

A: Tell me more about this.

S: I am not sure why I avoid difficult discussions. I have always done it to some extent. When I was with my erstwhile employer, I did not directly interact with the founder because—and this is my perception—he felt that I had interpersonal issues with him. Instead, the firm hired a senior leader who would function sort of like an intermediary.

A: Avoidance can be very useful at times; it depends on the context and how important the issue at hand is, and how important the relationship is.

There is a framework on conflict management that you might find interesting, it lets you explore different approaches to challenging interactions, based on the project and relationship importance. I will send it your way. It is based on the Thomas–Kilmann conflict resolution model.[5] I plan to also email you an article on the 'how to' when it comes to stressful conversations.

S: Thank you, that is great.

(**A's reflections:** Leaders rarely complete all the work they can do on their personal leadership in the typical six-to-twelve-month time frame that most coaching engagements span. Developing leadership skills is often a lifelong journey. It is not surprising that Saurabh may have grown leaps and bounds when it comes to managing his emotional resilience and ability to control his emotional outbursts. He also had moved forward when it comes to creating a more authentic professional setting for himself. However, his next step would be to move away from his limited approaches in the face of conflict and to use a framework to approach interpersonal challenges and the 'how' of having constructive conversations in difficult circumstances.

Secondly, learning and growth should happen during a coaching session. However, I would argue that a big chunk of learning takes place in between sessions when the client reflects on the conversation and reviews material the coach has shared with him. This 'in-between sessions' space is also where the client can test his assumptions about the world and experiment with new behaviours. The latter frequently offers rich material for subsequent sessions, where these new experiences can be reviewed by coach and client and learnings can be cemented. In general, sharing theoretical resources and frameworks is helpful, but as one of Saurabh's top strengths is Love of Learning, we have a particular lever for growth here, as he generally finds this theoretical part energizing.)

Excerpt 2, May 2022 via Zoom

A: Saurabh, among other things we discussed last time—that you tend to go into a 'tell' mode with others and do not ask as many questions about the other party's needs and thoughts as you could. This risks being a missed opportunity to negotiate well, as humans are poor mind readers. If you allow me, I want to use our coach–client relationship to illustrate this point. At one point we had explored my coming in and supporting you and the team as a board member. We had some back-and-forth on this subject and then the conversation seemed to just end. What do you make of that?

(**A's reflections**: I am aware that I have a certain sense of unease as I bring up this moment of unresolved matter between

Saurabh and myself. While I have trained in having difficult conversations, I know that I still do not particularly enjoy them.)

S: Yes, that was an interesting moment. I thought that your financial adviser's ask regarding how much we, as a team at Marcellus, should compensate you was not matching what we were thinking.

(**S's reflections**: For a moment, I am surprised that Ana brings this subject up. However, within seconds, another part of my brain tells me that by engaging me in a discussion on a difficult topic, Ana wants to walk me down a pathway that I am reluctant to explore. I, therefore, figure out that Ana wants to see whether I am making progress with my skill in having difficult discussions. That being said, I can feel myself getting uncomfortable—my throat is starting to feel dry as I know that my coach will now start pushing me mentally.)

A: So, instead of collaborating, we left it at this juncture without speaking further. Even though the issue at hand was important, so was the relationship. And, according to the model, we should have looked to stay in a collaborative space and find a win–win scenario. What was going through your mind at the time?

(**A's reflections**: This is an interesting moment in the conversation. In a phenomenological approach,[6] the coaching space and the coach-client relationship offer yet another opportunity to explore a client's struggle in a safe space and to generate insight that is useful beyond this very specific interaction.)

S: I did not want to offend you; you had offered such valuable coaching to me and the team at Marcellus.

(**S's reflections**: I am beginning to realize that even with people I like, my thinking ramps up when I sense a potential conflict or tension and it becomes less of a dialogue with the other person. I then risk going into a monologue and telling the other party what I think they want and how we will deal with it.)

A: I wonder what would have happened if you had asked me questions as to what was going on for me.

(**A's reflections**: I remember my own hesitation to push this topic at the time and finding myself in a space of wanting to accommodate and equally avoiding the difficult conversation. Here is a moment where I am not sure if I should share my thoughts or whether this is too much 'about me'. The key to sharing is that it serves one purpose and one purpose only: the client's agenda. I decide against offering this detail about my own process. And I continue to wonder: was it right to step away here?)

S: True, I did stay in my own head here as well.

A: Is there anything that you notice in your body as we are talking about this?

S: I noticed earlier that my throat was starting to feel dry.

(**S's reflections**: Now that Ana directs my attention away from my head to my body, I become acutely aware of other sensations as well, such as a certain tightness in my chest. In these Zoom sessions, to clearly hear what Ana is saying, I often turn off the air-conditioning. I feel beads of sweat forming on my forehead. But it is not only the heat. It is also a reminder of when I am in tricky business negotiations. I know this conversation is important. But this is also tough.)

(**A's reflections**: 'Embodiment' is an important part of the coaching work. It helps the client locate where he is mentally and emotionally by noticing what happens in his body. In this session, we address this more briefly, but there will be other sessions where we go deeper into this subject as it is important to regularly help clients identify their bodily sensations, as often the body signals emotion—such as distress, anger or joy—before we become conscious of it. Familiarity with one's physical reactions can help with mental self-regulation as well as allow the client to leverage the power of the mind-body connection more effectively.)

A: In general, we identified that you seem to avoid not only challenging interactions with people you dislike but also with people you do like. And while for the former you either delegate contact or avoid direct contact altogether, for the latter you tend to interact, but mostly on your own terms and more in a 'tell' mode. Have you been able to think about this some more?

S: Yes, I thought about this more and noticed that this is true; I seem to turn my curiosity mostly towards an internal dialogue as I prepare for these conversations. I sort of wonder about what the other person might want and prepare accordingly. But maybe that is because I am an introvert.

(**S's reflections**: This is an interesting insight, that avoidance is present irrespective of whether I like someone or not. At this point of the session, I also remember feeling like this is getting really tough and my brain wants to shut down. Here it is again, in this coaching session, me wanting to avoid discomfort. There is also a moment of levity as I catch myself being a bit cheeky and trying to lead Ana down a different route; introversion might be a good one?)

A: Introversion is an interesting angle; I am glad you bring this up. Introverts can indeed have significant internal dialogues; they tend to enjoy in-depth reflections. However, that does not mean that they cannot use curiosity when it comes to interacting with others. Extroverts often tend to seek lighter dialogue with a greater number of people. Introverts often enjoy a more in-depth conversation, one person at a time. So, I would argue that your introversion is not holding you back from asking pertinent questions. Maybe even to the contrary . . .

S: Hmmmm. Yes, I guess it comes back to the 'why' of me avoiding difficult conversations with others in general. As I think back to my time at my erstwhile employer, I remember that whenever 'bonus payment' time came around, I would ask HR to share the details with the team and I would go on holiday on that day. This way I would not have to deal with some of the frustrations that would emerge. And when I would return, if people were still upset with their bonuses, I would go into my second mode, I would shout at them and tell them to work harder so they could get a better bonus next time.

(S's reflections: Ana did not really take the bait of introversion that I inserted. We are right back on track. As I said, this is why I find my coaching sessions with her useful. It is a mental workout for the trickiest situations that I can face as a leader . . .)

A: Let's have a look at the framework on conflict I shared with you last time. Which of the five quadrants[7] were you operating in?

S: Looks like I was mostly in the avoidance or competition quadrant! Avoid when I can, and push for my agenda when I need to.

(S's reflections: There is a certain relief when I can tackle a problem intellectually. It feels familiar, all the way back to the time as an adolescent when I escaped to the library to avoid the tension around me.)

A: I agree. How do you manage the bonus situation at Marcellus today?

S: I have thought about this a lot over the past four years. As a result of these past experiences, I have asked my colleagues to come up with a bonus structure that we all can stand behind. Now, when bonus time rolls around, we all know what to expect and there is full transparency around what everyone is receiving as it is based on an algorithm we have collectively agreed on. So, looking at the framework, it seems like I am now operating more frequently in a collaborative framework. And I can see that I used accommodation for some contexts where I care about the person and the issue at hand was not critical for me.

(**S's reflections**: I have learnt that the world is imperfect and that I can't just go in and force my view on others. Leadership is about empowering the team and making space for others and their sensitivities.)

A: This is great, Saurabh. It looks like you have achieved greater progress than you had originally admitted to when we started this conversation. Bravo! Also, it seems like you have leveraged another one of your signature strengths, Creativity, as you came up with a new bonus approach.

(**A's reflections**: This intervention—like so many coaching interventions—can seem trivial. But it is deliberate and important that I as the coach highlight for Saurabh that he has successfully used more of the strategies for approaching conflict than he may have realized. Clients with a stentorian inner critic like Saurabh need to see the coach role model, that positive voice of acknowledgement. Coaching is not only about challenge; it is just as much about support. The idea is to raise a client's awareness so that he can eventually begin to internalize that external third-party voice. Given that most inner critics develop in childhood and adolescence, we are dealing with a very established voice usually, and many interventions by the coach are needed to firmly establish the client's inner balance of a positive mindset versus a critical mindset.)

Excerpt 3, May 2022 via Zoom

A: Saurabh, I would like to come back to the theme of avoidance that we identified during our last session. Is that okay?

S: Yes, good idea. To expand on this, I would like to explore what takes place when I face a party that I do not feel connected with. Maybe an example here is a good idea. At Marcellus, our financial products are distributed through intermediaries in the wealth management space. These distributors take a percentage of sales of our product as a fee for their services. Customary percentage cuts are 60 to 70 per cent of revenues in favour of the distributor, that is, for every $100 of revenues earned by the fund management house, the distributor takes $60–70 . . . Here we have entered interesting territory for tension, as at Marcellus we do not agree with this fee-sharing construct. We have decided as a firm to stick to a 50 per cent split between the distributor and us. Distributors who have agreed to sell our product have to accept the 50–50 split. Part of our relationship-building efforts with the distributors involves meeting them over a meal or a drink and interacting with them on a regular basis. Pramod, my fellow founder, tackles this aspect of our business. Pramod can leverage his strong relationship skills, which is also something he enjoys. I focus on areas of product development, a space where I feel energized.

A: Let's bring in again our Thomas–Kilmann model. Given that the intermediary needs to take a cut in their margin, this seems to be an example of a competitive approach where you get what you want. And you get what you want because Marcellus's products are being asked for by the end consumer. There is also the element of 'stepping away', where you delegate to your colleague Pramod. Since each of you gets to play to your strengths, this is a good example of when 'avoidance' can be a useful strategy. It shows that approaches to conflict are highly contextual. What would be a good example where avoidance may not be useful?

S: There is an important stakeholder in the industry whom I have refused to deal with, even though I know it is important for our long-term business expansion and I know that he will want to directly deal with me. He is an Alpha and only wants to talk to me as I am the largest shareholder in Marcellus. So, based on the framework you shared, the issue at hand is important for Marcellus and the relationship is important. I know this calls for a collaborative approach, and yet I have been avoiding him.

(**A's reflections:** I notice that here Saurabh has the laugh of a boy who has just been caught red-handed skipping school, knowing well he shouldn't. Often, our behaviours in the present are products of our past. Many of the stakeholders I interviewed for Chapter 5 mentioned Saurabh's rebellious side, keen to escape authority, starting with avoiding his mother's directives. I am making a mental note of this, as we will need to distinguish between what is harmless mischief that many of us display at times and what are the moments where his rebellious attitude to authority harms him, as a leader and as a person.)

A: What is the reason for this avoidance?

S: He has a big ego, is an Alpha and wants to be treated accordingly.

(**S's reflections**: This question makes me reflect deeper. There is an emotional reaction in me when I face people I dislike. My brain seems to say, '*I just don't want to deal with this guy.*' There is another part of me, a more practical one, that says, '*Get over yourself and connect with this guy for the sake of getting results.*' So, I guess there is also an inner conflict that is taking place inside my head.)

A: This seems to trigger you. What value of yours might be behind this?

S: I think it is probably a sense of fairness and respect. Respect needs to be earned.

(**A's reflections**: Note here that parents, another Alpha role, often demand respect from their children without 'earning' it necessarily. I wonder how much of Saurabh is still rebelling against his parents that he gets triggered by Alphas in business.)

A: It feels like you may be in your own head again. What do you know about this Alpha, and what else do you want or need to know about him? I wonder if it could be helpful if you knew about what matters to him, what keeps him up at night?

(**A's reflections**: I decide to explore the here-and-now and come back to Saurabh's currently limited use of one of his great strengths: Curiosity. Collaboration requires that we first understand what the other party needs and that we ask questions rather than run with our assumptions. Here, I am asking several questions in a row. The idea is to suggest areas he could get curious about.)

S: Hmmm . . . true. I am again in my own head.

A: Here is a challenge for you to get yourself out of your own head: set up a meeting with that Alpha, and during that meeting, your task is to find out as much as you can about him, his aspirations, concerns, long-term plans, core values and so forth. Bring what you learn as part of this experiment back to our coaching space. Also, if you can note down what, if anything, you notice when it comes to changes within yourself vis-à-vis this Alpha. Do your assumptions about him hold up, does something shift; if yes, what in particular and why? Does that sound okay?

S: Yes, this sounds interesting, I will give this a shot.

Excerpt 4, May 2022 via Zoom

S: I have done quite some research and have discovered that this stakeholder has a significant Achilles heel in his business model. I set up a video-call with him and shared with him a solution to this conundrum and he was very impressed, and we have started building more of a relationship.

(A's reflections: Here, I need to be agile as the coach. This was not the way the homework had been intended. Instead of— as part of the experiment—sitting down with the other party and directly getting to know them better, Saurabh had used his strength of curiosity and explored the stakeholder's business. To be fair, he did accept the challenge to connect with the Alpha and set up a conversation to discuss the finding of his free-of-charge research. However, he introduced an element of transaction, where he offers 'free advice' in exchange for a better relationship. Also, by increasing his knowledge about his counterpart's business, does he wish to minimize ambiguity, another strategy to assume a form of control?

Avoidance seems to be a theme here also. Yet, while as coaches we need to nudge our clients out of their comfort zone, sometimes a baby step in the right direction is better than a big leap, which may turn out to be too substantial to be sustained. Saurabh seemed energized by his variation of the homework. What I noticed as well was that he had used his strength of Creativity, which had come in handy. The result was close to what we had intended: he was, in fact, interacting with a challenging counterpart in a collaborative manner and seemed engaged in the process. One step at a time. I am making a mental note to invite Saurabh to approach the stakeholder in other ways. For now, I will see how I can help him build on his forward movement.)

A: I see that you have used some important influencing or movement techniques such as reciprocity and expertise here as you are looking to collaborate. This is great. When I trained as a mediator, we summarized some key techniques; would you be interested in having a copy?

S: That would be great. I will read this on one of my upcoming flights.

*

Managing relationships is a lifelong journey, for leaders and for people in general. There are further conversations to be had. Let's stop here. Saurabh is moving forward nicely, step by step. As part of our work in 2017, Saurabh had successfully moved away from getting emotionally hijacked.[8] And on the rare occasion when he feels the old demon raise its head, he manages to rein it in. Sometimes he will step away from conflict as it becomes heated. Here, avoidance can be a good strategy as it helps to protect the relationship: it allows him to cool down emotionally and come back to the issue once he feels calm and collected.

Avoidance in its less constructive form has also emerged as a theme when it comes to Saurabh. In part, it was always there in him. As a little boy, he was always out and about, away from the gaze of his mother, in search of adventure. This rebellious streak of not going by the rules has stayed with him and in many ways has served him well. He veered off the path of conformity very early in his life, and his professional success speaks for itself. Yet, like all of us, Saurabh can expand his repertoire and does not need to stay stuck in just one way of doing things. As his awareness rises, so does his ability to make intentional choices as to how to act. By learning different techniques to manage stressful conversations, such as being clear in his messaging, and adopting neutrality and temperance in his delivery, he is on his way. By tapping more intentionally into his signature strengths of Curiosity and Creativity, he will be able to manage difficult conversations with greater ease and create win-win outcomes for all involved.

I know that as part of my role and responsibility as a coach, I need to sometimes challenge and confront clients with tough realities. Over the years, I have developed a good sense as to how to do that and, equally, how to balance challenge with support for the client. Saurabh is naturally courageous and keen to learn, so he will be pushing himself year after year. The key is here that we regularly introduce moments of recognition, of pause, and also of encouragement to offer him these pockets of support.

Key Takeaways

- The essence of this book is revealed: the reader peeks behind the door of a real coaching session. What is confidential becomes public. Here is the opportunity for anyone interested in hiring a coach to 'touch' what it feels like to be in a session. And the opportunity for coaches to compare best practices and what they might want to integrate into their own work as well as what not to.

- What's more: coach and client also reveal what is not being said in the coaching session. Readers get to review intimate reflections of inner dialogues, revealing vulnerabilities and self-doubts as well as intentional choices to withhold certain thoughts.

- Readers also get the chance to reflect on what choices they would have made in a given moment of the session and compare this to what actually happened. How might a different course of action have changed the outcome?

- 'Embodiment' is an important part of the coaching work. It helps the client locate where he is mentally and emotionally by noticing what happens in his body. Familiarity with one's physical reactions can help with mental self-regulation as well, as it allows the client to leverage the power of the mind-body connection more effectively.

- A big chunk of learning takes place in between sessions where the client reflects on the conversations and reviews material the coach has suggested.

When you read, don't just consider what the author thinks, consider what you think. You must strive to find your own voice. Thoreau said, 'Most men lead lives of quiet desperation.' Don't be resigned to that. Break out. Don't just walk off the edge like lemmings. Look around you. Strike out and find new grounds. Compose a poem of your own.

John Keating (Robin Williams) from _Dead Poets Society_ (1989)

Stay Curious, My Friends
Ana's reflections

When Saurabh convinced me to collaborate on this book, I was all in. First, my dream all those years ago as a rookie coach was to be a fly on the wall in a professional coaching room. So, this would be my invitation to give emerging coaches what I once wished to have. Of course, not all the decisions we make in life are entirely altruistic, especially those that take away a large portion of our time, like writing this book. In daring to write alongside Saurabh, I felt that I would also learn more about myself and my practice. This 'indirect education' would help me grow as a coach and maybe even become wiser as a person.

As Chapter 7 reflects on what we have produced, we decided to save it for last and only to write it once we had read each other's preceding chapters. On reading my co-author's observations of me, joy and gratitude filled my heart. Nevertheless, a part of me felt apprehensive when I read his tributes. It knew that the only way off a pedestal was down. And I knew that Saurabh was reading the reality of my experience at the same time—and finding out that I am not the perfect sage who has all the answers but a fallible human prone to the same anxieties that she addresses in her clients. I wondered if the revelation of this 'other side' of my character might affect our working relationship forever.

Adam I and Adam II: two sides to human nature

For me, character is ultimately about multiples—in life, you will rarely find a personality that is entirely one thing or another. I feel this book represents these multiple sides of human beings that sometimes compete with each other but ultimately comprise a more profoundly human sense of being. We try to mask those parts of our personality that we believe are less attractive to others or, when it comes to business, less fitting with the company culture. In *The Lonely Man of Faith*, Rabbi Joseph Soloveitchik is concerned with exactly this issue of the public and hidden 'sides' to human nature when he reflects on the philosophical problem of the two accounts of Adam's creation in the Book of Genesis.[1] Soloveitchik contends that these 'two Adams' stood for the two opposing sides of human nature, and names them Adam I and Adam II. His essay argues that most of us feel the tension between these two sides of ourselves.

Adam I represents our public, outward-facing side. In the context of coaching, Adam I seeks success. He aims to achieve this through measurable results. For Adam I, status and tangible accomplishments are everything. This Adam is fiercely competitive and ready to impress the world. The ambitions of Adam I will naturally resonate with many executive coaching clients.

Adam II represents our inner character. In our context of business coaching, we might define Adam II as not only doing good work but also *being* a good colleague. This latter side is more flexible in its approach to life. For Adam I, failure is a disaster best avoided. But Adam II sees failure as an opportunity to learn and to acknowledge that our ideas won't always work out the way we might want them to. Adam II's integrity and inner reflection enable him to resist Adam I's temptation to seek rewards. Instead, Adam II chooses to follow his moral compass. To Adam II, other people matter, but in the sense that he can help and support them rather than use them to promote himself. Ultimately, Adam II seeks meaningful existence and a type of existential truth. In the business world, Adam II represents the desire to collaborate, support others and reveal one's honest, fallible self to others for connection.

The corporate world thinks it needs lots and lots of Adam Is. Many businesspeople believe this too. Most of my senior clients start out by looking at our coaching exchange through a utilitarian lens. They will ask themselves, *'What's in it for me? What do I have to do to be rewarded with more prestige, a promotion, better business results?'* Saurabh was no different. As you learnt in Chapter 3, he chose me over the other coach purely because it appeared that I would make the process easy for him. The coaching process was a means to an end—to help him play the 'corporate game'.

Of course, Adam I is necessary in the corporate world. But to my mind, good executive coaching (and thus business practice) does not stop at the extrinsic rewards for which Adam I hunts. The best—and ultimately the most rewarding—coaching *starts* there. Adam Is might make for a prosperous world, but it won't necessarily be a happy world. Adam II is also needed for balance, to foster and maintain positive energy and engagement among people. This is harder to achieve because a client who has been taught only to seek Adam I is unlikely to be interested in finding their Adam II. But this step is crucial for maintaining positive change.

In addition to helping the coachee achieve the goals that his Adam I desires, the coach must also tease Adam II out of their clients. As clients might be resistant to Adam II, a coach must first create a trusting space in which Adam II can feel safe to enter. When coaching, I do this using the methods explored in this book, the most important of them being carefully listening to the client and the people around them. In this sense, I believe Saurabh and I have achieved such a feat in writing this book. We have revealed our weaknesses as well as our strengths, and this humility—our Adam II—only serves to make us better-rounded people, both personally and professionally.

Not all those who wander are lost

The other important lesson the co-authoring of this book has imparted to me is that we must be open to adventure and delve into the unknown because these moments afford us deep reflection. I witnessed some of these moments in the figurative mirror that Saurabh held up to my coaching. In this sense, the journey has become a teacher for both of us. I have been able to visualize my own story and to look deeper into my own actions rather than merely respond to my client's, and I have found this a genuinely satisfying and rewarding way to think about how I might adapt my coaching style to the varying needs of my clients.

As with many adventures, it helps to have a map. Through our working relationship, it has been vital that I, as the coach, am aware of the context surrounding my client. Just as it's helpful to know where to expect a river blocking our path, and where we will need to get out our climbing equipment to traverse a mountain range. Understanding how clients feel beyond the scope of our coaching sessions is essential to realizing what their experience of the journey is and making recommendations for their improvement. A client's reactions during our sessions can be due to projection or transference, something they have drawn from experience. It is also essential to know this, as you can then avoid triggering the client unexpectedly. Such dynamics are well documented in the literature on human functioning, and they are also important concepts for executive coaches to understand.

Acceptance is the beginning of change

I have thought a great deal about the outcome of this book and what a reader might learn from it. The reader's and author's takeaways will ultimately boil down to the same notion: that lasting change is only possible when we can embrace our imperfections.

Yet, facing this reality can be tricky, even for seasoned coaches, and this issue doubles in magnitude when we disclose our imperfections to our clients, who, after all, trust us with handling their own fallibility. Some colleagues who learnt that I was writing a book with a client reacted with concern as to how I would balance writing with my professional work, and even with incredulity: why would I, at this stage of my career, after having built a strong brand and credibility, risk jeopardizing it all by revealing my innermost reflections?

All these concerns are reasonable and human. Nevertheless, serving as a role model doesn't need to mean I must be perfect. In fact, if we adopt the Adam I/Adam II analogy, the opposite will more often be true. The necessary qualities for a human being include courage, motivation, empathy and acceptance. In other words, a healthy balance of our two sides.

This book has been the perfect realization of my Adam II, as it has challenged me not to 'hide behind' accreditations, affiliations and my client list. Yes, throughout my work with Saurabh, I was keen to help him navigate his corporate goals and cultivate his professional skills. But, at the same time, I aimed to encourage self-exploration, empathy and humility in him. Not every leader will accept such an invitation, because not every leader will be flexible in changing her intrinsic motivations and goals.

The mystery of life should be celebrated

In the year we wrote this book, Saurabh opened up more than he ever did before and he began to trust me to speak to those closest to him. I came to see a much better-rounded character relative to the Saurabh I first met in 2017. I have had the privilege to be sad with him for his losses, to feel uplifted by his belief in a better future, and to admire his energy and determination to create that future. And I have felt a deep friendship emerge, one that I look forward to seeing blossom in the years to come.

Writing this book has revealed much, yet it cannot definitively answer *why* our partnership worked.[2] Nevertheless, I believe that an element of mystery is important—it keeps us going. I believe that the more open we can be about the aspects of ourselves we usually keep hidden, and the more flexible we are to exploring a path where we might not be sure of the outcome, the better off we will be. This takes courage, as society and the business world often tell us to do the opposite—to be upfront about our achievements but secretive about the areas where we need support. A coach can help us set milestones along the way, give us the confidence to play to our strengths and acknowledge our weaknesses, and thus aim for a life of integrity.

Mystery is also much closer to our lived experience. We can't fit life into a series of labelled boxes. It is much healthier to provide for a margin of error and to be aware that there can't be 100 per cent certainty as to why something works between a client and coach. We must only remember to enjoy and fully experience that adventure by being open and trusting.

Saurabh's reflections

Looking back

As we entered the final chapter of this book, Ana and I separately reflected on the process of writing this book, what we have learnt from it and whether we have cracked the code of why our coaching partnership has been as successful as it has been. In parallel, I have also introspected on how the coaching journey, which began six years ago, has changed me (for more, see Chapter 3).

In my previous role, professional and personal pressures turned me into a taskmaster for my colleagues and my team. Thanks to hiring Ana as my coach, I came to realize after working with her that such a style of management seldom works when one is managing large teams of highly skilled professionals. Further, Ana helped me understand change needs to start from within myself. And that with certainty about who one is as a person and who one aspires to be as a leader comes the confidence to begin implementation of the appropriate changes—both in the context of the self and in the context of the world around us. Reaching this conclusion in the early months of 2018 was one of the turning points of my career.

As I designed the next chapter of my career and founded Marcellus Investment Managers in 2018, the mental pathways that Ana helped me see made me perceive opportunities where previously I might have seen only obstacles. In the spring of

2020, when COVID-19 hammered our financial position, my colleagues and I, through Ana's coaching of the team, were able to pick ourselves up and move forward as a group. As Marcellus continues to grow at a rapid clip, I will look for Ana's coaching in the years to come to help me become the best version of myself, to be the strong leader that my team deserves.

And so, you may ask, after reflecting deeply on our journey and after writing this book together with my coach, how did I experience this process? And what have I learnt that will let me 'crack the code' of what made this coaching partnership a success?

The process

A bag of mixed emotions

A decade ago, when I was writing my third book, *The Unusual Billionaires*, one of India's most successful businessmen had given me some advice that my authentic self of today can fully appreciate. He told me, '*When you write a book, write what you would like to read. Do not try to second-guess what the wider world would like to read.*' After a few days of reflection, I realized that this was sound advice—it is only when we are our true selves that what we have to say can be of genuine interest to others. Therefore, as part of writing this book, I have tried to tap into my inner compass as much as possible. I can honestly say—to paraphrase Charles Dickens—that 'it was the best of times, it was the most challenging of times'. Writing this book has been an adventure that has supported my growth and teased me out of my comfort zone, much like the coaching Ana has done.

As I now know from Ana's coaching, I struggle to readily articulate my feelings when asked to tap into my inner world of reflections. And I am also aware of my tendency in those moments to want to mentally run off into intellectual analysis. So, you may ask, what did it make me feel, writing this book?

The early chapters of the book, especially Chapter 3, were hard to write—I had never written about myself before, and honestly did not know where to start. However, courtesy of Ana's nudges, I persisted. By the time we reached the final chapter, I was writing fluently and candidly about myself!

There were moments of stimulating creativity and of feeling engaged and alive, such as the brainstorming session (over another delicious sushi lunch in the Little Venice neighbourhood of London where Ana lives) that led to this chapter. There were times of laughter, such as when Ana discovered that I had hired her as she seemed to be the 'easy coach'. There was a sense of excitement when we ran our photo shoot for the book.

There were also moments of challenge. At times, I feared whether I was being too candid in my narrative. I was concerned that I might lose the respect of Marcellus's clients if they see that I am a fallible human being. I also wondered if one could truly capture the power of a coaching session in a written format (as we have done in Chapter 6), given that the reader is not privy to the tone of voice used, the gestures or the facial expressions, and cannot understand how much is left unsaid (but is implicitly communicated) in these sessions.

Overall, I am thrilled that Ana and I had this unique opportunity to explore and understand the coaching relationship in a way that has never been documented before. To my mind, that is what a fulfilling career is all about—taking your mind to places it has never been before and having experiences that help you become stronger, fitter and better.

I remain curious to see the world's reaction to this unique book.

The coaching relationship changed

For me, the work that Ana and I have done for the book has transformed the coach-client relationship, which is arguably a modern Western construct, into something more akin to what in Indian culture we would call the 'guru-shishya' relationship (crudely translated into English as the master-pupil relationship). In almost all east Asian and south Asian societies, the relationship between the master and the pupil is invested with immense psychological, sometimes even spiritual, significance. In the Asian context, and in the context of all of India's great religions, the master-pupil relationship is anything but transactional.

Tradition has it that this form of learning—rather than textbooks and classrooms—is the best way for subtle or advanced knowledge to be conveyed. Eventually, the student masters the knowledge that the guru embodies. As we structured the book and gave it granularity, colour and depth, I became very much the shishya, the pupil, marvelling at Ana's ability to keep asking question after question that illuminated the blind spots in my psyche and opened the path to strengthening my mind. My sincere hope is that every reader of this book can find their guru—a teacher, an adviser, a mentor, and a sounding board—as a high-achieving professional seeking to find his or her way in the world.

Lessons get reinforced

The process of writing this book has also reinforced some important key messages the initial coaching with Ana had brought to the surface. The most critical one, I believe, is my resilience and well-being in the here and now, as it directly impacts my ability to deliver as a leader and to create a culture of meaning and purpose for the future. Let me expand a bit on this. In the five years that I have worked with Ana, several of her psychological nudges have been aimed at getting me to reduce my self-neglect and spend more 'me time'. For several years now, some of my family—including my wife and my mother— have been asking me to slow down as well. Not dissimilar to my 360-degree feedback in 2017, the feedback today from people closest to me and their concerns about my strenuous work schedule raise the importance and urgency of righting this self-neglect (see Chapter 5).

As we discussed the material contained in this chapter, Ana pointed out to me the research done on this subject by the renowned psychologist Phillip Zimbardo. Zimbardo's work on this subject—which he titled 'The Time Perspective'—has helped me understand better both the drivers of my workaholism and how I can have a measure of control on the same.

Zimbardo's research illustrates three paradoxes about the concept of 'Time':[3]

- Time is one of the most powerful influences on our thoughts, feelings and actions, yet we are usually totally unaware of the effect of time in our lives.
- Each specific attitude toward time—or time perspective— is associated with numerous benefits, yet in excess, each is associated with even greater costs.
- Individual attitudes toward time are learnt through personal experience, yet collectively, attitudes toward time influence national destinies.[4]

By applying Zimbardo's model to my life, I have realized that as I grew up in the 1980s in Delhi and in the 1990s in London, my family's circumstances meant that very early on in life I had learnt that unless I focused on looking for a way out of the difficult circumstances we as a family were enduring and imagining a brighter future, all of our lives would remain mired in challenging circumstances. Secondly, my parents trained me explicitly to sacrifice jam today for jelly, chocolates and other desserts tomorrow. This is what Zimbardo calls being 'future focused'.

The combination of these two triggers—my own tendency to look forward rather than to worry about the present, and my parents' training—created a virtuous circle for me through my teenage years and into adulthood. I would first focus on a positive future outcome, say, becoming a market-leading equity analyst in whichever country I was living in at the time. I would then work hard to achieve this goal for a few years, sacrificing leisure time with loved ones, relaxation time for myself and sleep time. A few years later, I would hit the desired goal. As a result of the achievement, new horizons and opportunities would open up for my family and for myself. And you can guess what I would do next . . . That's right, I would choose an even more challenging goal, say, creating a market-leading asset management franchise in whichever country I was living in at that point, and the whole cycle would start all over again.

The profession I belong to—financial analysis and investing—rewards this sort of behaviour. People like me get paid to understand how a company will fare over the next ten to twenty years. For someone like me who was brought up from an early age to live for and feast on 'jelly tomorrow', this aspect of investment management works beautifully. In other words, I am paid by Marcellus's clients to live in the future.

Living and working like this means that my mind is constantly churning and is almost exclusively focused on the future. The upside of this is that I don't get particularly worried when I encounter challenges along the way. Very little in the 'here' and the 'now' preoccupies me, as I am already living in the future. This is extremely useful for me in my professional life because, if Marcellus's investments are underperforming for a few quarters, I don't fret and beat myself or my colleagues up; my colleagues and I stay 'future focused'. However, this does not mean it is all sweetness and sunshine in my life. The downside of being mainly future-focused is that it makes me feel disconnected from the world around me. In fact, thanks to our marriage of over twenty years, my wife has perfected the art of looking into my eyes for a fraction of a second and knowing when I am not in the present!

As Zimbardo points out, and as writing this book has reminded me, living too much in the future and too little in the present is not healthy. My challenge in the months and years ahead is to tilt my restless mind away from the future a little bit and towards the present a bit more.

Cracking the code (a little more)

Coming into my own

While writing this book, I stumbled upon the journal I had kept during my teens and twenties. Halfway through the journal, I found something that I had written thirty years ago as an undergraduate student at the LSE:

When a single voice cries out in the dark, listen to that voice. Listen to what it has to say. When a single light emerges out of the darkness, walk towards it. Be guided by your conscience. Be guided by God and goodness. Walk in the darkness knowing that there are pitfalls. Try to reach the source of the voice, the source of the light. Then use the light and the voice to guide you through the darkness and out into the day.

As soon as I read what I had journalled three decades ago, I felt a key had been slipped into a lock.

As a student, I was keenly conscious of the contrast between the cocky, confident, extroverted persona that I put on to succeed in the wider world, and the conscientious, thoughtful, introverted person that I became when I was either by myself or with people I loved. I used to struggle to reconcile these two personas. I did courses where I was taught how to improve my presentation skills. I attended lectures where 'leadership skills' were taught. I tried to wear nice clothes. And I listened to others telling me to do things that rich, 'grown-up' people do: cultivate a taste for golf, wear expensive watches, drink fine wine and buy expensive cars. Yet, my idea of a good time was relaxing at an empty beach in Goa, my head buried in a book, sipping a gin and tonic,[5] with my better half at my side.

When Ana entered the picture five years ago, she helped me understand that, given my skillsets, if I could focus on becoming more of who I am (rather than pretending to be someone who wasn't me), things would more or less start falling into place. I reckon the first six months of my working with Ana were fundamentally about this realization—that I could give myself permission to play to my strengths and values. Couching it in the language of my journal from thirty years ago, my dialogue with Ana became the light that was dragging me out of the night and into the day. For highly strung professionals like me who can spend months wrestling with specific moral and ethical dilemmas, having such a voice to turn to can be immensely beneficial. This aspect of coaching, which is non-remedial (i.e., in this context, the coach is not fixing a specific problem or person but is instead acting as a sounding board, deeply listening, offering advice where appropriate and focusing on your authenticity and strengths), is an important distinction I had no understanding of—until Ana and I started writing this book.

A growth mindset in relationships

The year spent writing this book has allowed me to understand human strengths—not just Ana's and mine but also of the rest of the people around us—in a different light. Rather than seeing myself and the people around me as a fixed collection of skills and abilities, I have understood more clearly how we can help each other become more skilful professionals and more fulfilled human beings.

I have learnt to use the influence Ana has had on me as a parable of how I can influence other people. I think I have begun to understand how relationships, which at the outset might appear transactional—be it a coaching relationship, or the kind of relationship I have with Marcellus's clients—might deepen into not just friendship but also skills and knowledge. Since, like Ana, I know several people who are thinkers and doers of repute, this opens up for me a whole new world of possibilities.

As illustrated in the dialogues in Chapter 6 where Ana is coaching me on how to have difficult conversations, I, in turn, can help other professionals in my field of work—namely, investment. However, I also remembered something that my paternal grandmother told me when I became a teenager: '*Never give uncalled-for advice.*' So, I asked myself, '*How can I help other professionals in my line of work without their feeling that this is uncalled-for advice?*' The answer: join forces with other investors and set up a trade body for portfolio managers in India. And thus the Association of Portfolio Managers in India (APMI) was born, as we were midway through writing this book. APMI now has over 110 members who handle nearly 90 per cent of the assets managed in India by portfolio managers.

Looking ahead

I saw my parents work very hard—first in India, and then in the UK—to give my sister and me the best life they could. Since Sarbani and I have known each other since our primary school days, I had seen her parents do the same too. Until late in their careers, both sets of parents would wake up very early in the morning and set off to work. I have seen my mum in London and Sarbani's dad in Delhi return home at 10 p.m. until very late in their working lives. For their generation, work-life balance was not something the employer offered.

As I entered my late teens and understood how much it cost to feed, clothe and educate two teenagers, I realized just how hard both sets of parents had worked to give their children a good life. That understanding has had a profound influence on how I have thought about what money means to me—not so much a means to buy the good things in life for myself but a means to give my family the best that I can. And therefore, Sarbani and I try to do whatever we can to ensure that our kids will grow into confident, self-aware adults who are comfortable in their skin and proud of their roots. Having learnt from our upbringing that killing yourself to come first in every exam is not necessarily the optimal path to a happy adulthood, we try to achieve a balance between ensuring that the children focus on their academics and cultivate other interests (baking and writing in Malini's case and music and football in Jeet's case). We hope, as parents, that a decade hence, both our children will have found their place in the world. When I am not thinking about Marcellus, I spend most of my time thinking about how we can help our kids navigate their teenage years. I am sure Sarbani and I are no different from other parents in this regard.

My second set of aspirations is for Marcellus. In 2008, Sarbani and I moved from London to India because we felt that India would, over the rest of our lives, develop in the topsy-turvy fashion of America in the seventy years prior to the Second World War. The combination of railroads, the telegraph and the motor car, alongside a democratic political system and a free-market economy, made America the world's most powerful economy by the time the Second World War ended. Having studied economic history at LSE, I applied my knowledge of history to India and believed that India too can follow a similar trajectory as America in its pre-War years. Thankfully, we haven't been wrong in our assessment of India in this regard. Over the past decade, the Indian highway network has doubled, the number of bank accounts trebled, the number of brokerage accounts quadrupled, local airline traffic pentupled and broadband connectivity has grown forty-fold. The combination of this dynamic economy and Marcellus's talented team is intoxicatingly powerful—basically, we have combined the world's most happening economy with 120 highly accomplished and driven professionals. A decade hence, I see Marcellus as an asset management company that allows millions of Indians to enhance their wealth by investing— through Marcellus—in the booming Indian economy.

I work hard because I enjoy the intellectual challenge that leading an asset management business is. However, managing a rapidly growing asset management firm also brings with it other challenges. For example, our clients are spread not just across the vast expanse of India but also across the USA, the UK, the Middle East and the Far East. As a result, even in this post-COVID age of videoconferencing, running Marcellus entails my travelling every week. During these trips, while I try my best to keep up with my exercise schedule (my yoga instructor uses Zoom to ensure that I don't cheat on my schedule), my back plays up every now and then, as if to tell me that at some stage a decade hence, I will have to take my foot off the pedal.

Therefore, my fellow founders and I are grooming the next generation of leaders at Marcellus, and a decade hence, I will pass on the baton to the next generation. As I am sure you can imagine, this change of guard at Marcellus will bring with it a separate set of challenges and opportunities.

What will I do when I am done with my career in the financial markets? Provided that our families are financially secure when I call time on my professional career, Sarbani and I are keen that we do whatever we can to give back to India. At this stage, I am not sure how much of this giving back will be just financial and how much of it will consist of our applying our minds and bodies to specific causes. While we hope to be involved in specific causes, India is not a country for the faint-hearted. The Indian political and legal system can be ruthless and seemingly arbitrary, especially if you upset the myriad vested interests who control the levers of power in the country. Therefore, this is like a game of chess—to which I will apply my mind over the next decade or so. But such challenges are what make life worth living. And I am confident that Ana will be there to help me navigate these crossroads yet to come.

Key Takeaways

- For executive coaching to be impactful and meaningful, it needs to facilitate both extrinsic Adam I goals (ambition, status, tangible accomplishments) as well as intrinsic Adam II goals (seeking connection, collaboration, being authentic). In bridging the tension between Adam I and Adam II and offering ways to combine doing well with doing good, this is where we see clients flourish.
- While writing this book, the boundaries between client and coach were pushed, and it was our openness to adventure and to delving into the unknown that generated moments of

insight for both client and coach, such as that transformative change takes longer than one thinks (usually years), small things can move the needle and we need to remain attentive to them, and the relationship between coach and client is the foundation for any successful change.

- The coach-client relationship can be described, in Eastern philosophy, as the 'guru-shishya' (master-pupil) relationship. Indian tradition has it that this form of learning—rather than textbooks and classrooms—is the best way for subtle or advanced knowledge to be conveyed. Eventually, the student masters the knowledge that the guru embodies.

- A growth mindset (as opposed to a fixed mindset) is where we are prepared to take on challenges, where we can get better through hard work, embrace failure as learning opportunities, and ask for support and feedback from others.

- Curiosity remains a superpower. It facilitates innovation, creativity, health and well-being. As long as we are curious, we will see growth happen, in ourselves and others.

APPENDIX 1

Resources

Chapter 1: What to look for in a coach

Desirable qualifications, traits and experience to look for

Experience and Background

- Business training and a generally strong grasp of the principles of leadership (ideally, the coach has led teams before).
- A robust working knowledge of the client's industry, organization and the client's role within it.
- Psychological training and a robust understanding of human development.
- Coaching training, and a full understanding of coaching best practices.
- Ability to gauge overall fit and client motivation, and insight as to when to refer the client to another coach.
- Awareness of their own limits: A solid grasp of where coaching has its limits and where other interventions (such as therapy) might be better suited.
- Ability to identify patterns that can help the client develop insights to support his own progress.

- Willingness to show flexibility for last-minute priorities and integrate those with the client's long-term objectives.
- Focuses on clients' strengths and independence, and through building confidence, supports them in completing their coaching.

Approach

- Establishes and upholds a framework based on solid ground rules, confidentiality and a coaching process that is conducive to the client's ability to develop, learn and grow.
- Creates clarity and alignment between the client and key stakeholders on achievable objectives, milestones and the need for specific resources.
- Designs a bespoke process that will lead to the desired outcome and meet the needs of the client.
- Adjusts to changing circumstances and goalposts during the engagement.
- Remains accessible throughout the engagement and in between scheduled sessions.
- Provides resources that will accelerate the client's learning curves and progress.
- Supports, challenges and holds clients accountable in the matter of agreed-upon deliverables.

Mindset

- Puts the client first.
- Strictly adheres to confidentiality agreements. Strong ethical conduct, delivering work with integrity.
- Adopts a growth mindset. Believes that all clients have tappable resources for development, that they can evolve,

and that attitudes and behaviours can be modified or transformed.

- Holds the client in positive regard. Coach is non-judgemental and welcomes what the client wants to bring into their shared space.
- Empathetic to what it feels like to be the client, and to perceive the world as the client perceives it. The coach accurately reflects back to the client what they heard from the client.
- Manages boundaries and only shares information upon express permission from the client.

Chapter 2: Define your compass

How many boring PowerPoint presentations have you been through? Today's business world focuses on charts, data and facts. We are keen to make good, 'rational' decisions, and anecdotes seem to have little place in that. And yet, we do know that emotions are the music of leadership and that stories, not raw data, are what move people. The best leaders are also often great storytellers. They tell themselves the right stories that help them be true to themselves and their values. They also know how to engage those around them with a narrative that creates a sense of shared purpose and direction and inspires alignment on how to overcome challenges.

Stories do not need to be long to bring a message across. Hemingway's shortest story makes this clear: 'Baby shoes, never worn, for sale.' Stories need to move us, invite us to reflect, and possibly call us to action. The best stories are based on experience and observations and are not necessarily amusing or clever.

Exercise 1: Tell your story backwards

Consider the following: imagine it is your ninety-fifth birthday; you are sitting on your veranda and all the people that mattered in your life are there. They are standing in groups on the front lawn.

1. Who is there?

Now, get up and start walking around, and just listen in on their conversations.

2. What do you hope they say about you? What do you want to hear?

Look at yourself today.

3. How much of how you live and what you lead today is moving you towards that ninety-fifth-birthday conversation you hope to hear?
4. What do you need to do more of, what less of, and what to stop doing, to make sure you will create your desired legacy?

Exercise 2: Tell your story now and forward

Step 1

What are your top three personal values (for example, being genuine, adventuresome, focused)? How do these values come to life in your day-to-day interactions with others?

We have provided below a list of common values and their definitions. Please feel free to select your top three values from these lists to shape your 'Who Am I' story. Please do not feel limited by this list and come up with your own set of values for the purpose of the exercise.

1. Authenticity: Being true to yourself and to your values and encouraging this in your team to build relationships based on trust.
2. Autonomy: Giving freedom and responsibility to your team, trusting them to make the right decisions and guiding them through mistakes.
3. Boldness: Creating an atmosphere that rewards risk-taking, goal-setting and getting things done despite adversities.
4. Compassion: Being sympathetic to others, especially those facing challenges, by being patient and kind instead of judgemental.
5. Curiosity: An innate desire to keep learning, to know more about something; helps in approaching tough situations with an open mind.
6. Empowerment: Believing in the abilities of your team and providing them with the means and systems to accomplish their goals.
7. Faith: A strong belief, confidence and trust—often without proof or fact—in something (like a cause) and/or someone.
8. Fairness: Treating everyone fairly and justly without letting your feelings get in the way; stems from the belief that everyone should get a fair chance or opportunity.
9. Growth: Overcoming challenges, achieving higher goals by staying positive, improving, and growing your talents over time.
10. Happiness: Staying positive and hopeful despite life's many uncertainties and challenges; embracing happiness as a mindset and not a goal.
11. Honesty: Being true to yourself and to others, believing in and living life with virtues such as integrity and sincerity.

12. Leadership: Making sound decisions; the ability to influence and inspire others to perform well and to move towards the achievement of a common goal.
13. Loyalty: Staying firm and faithful to yourself and your team, creating an atmosphere that fosters dedication to key principles and/or people.
14. Optimism: An open-minded belief in positive outcomes and that matters can and will go well. Optimism links well with perseverance, dedication and commitment.
15. Patience: Having the capacity to accept and tolerate challenges in the path of doing your work. Being patient means being calm despite odds and adversity.
16. Peace: Accepting and addressing conflict without resorting to confrontation and believing in harmony and unity.
17. Reputation: Believing in how and what your brand is perceived as and presented to stakeholders. Reputations have an intangible value that is earned over time.
18. Spirituality: Separate from religion, spirituality means believing that life has meaning and purpose and that you have an inner and higher self (spirit) along with your physical body.
19. Trust: Synonymous with belief in the reliability and truth of people and values. Trust is the starting point and foundation of any relationship.
20. [Insert your value/s here]

Step 2

Personal values develop over a lifetime, and you will likely find evidence of this in your past. Take one value dear to you. Now consider the four experiences below as you develop your story that shares something meaningful about yourself with respect to this value.

➤ A time in your life when this value was challenged
➤ A person or event that taught you the importance of this value
➤ A time when you fell short of your own expectations
➤ A movie/story/event that exemplifies this value for you

Start to write your story in a 'stream of consciousness' style, not editing yourself. Simply 'upload' the memory in the order it occurs to you, documenting as much sensory data as possible— smells, tastes, touch, sounds, scene detail and dialogue. Write uninterrupted for five minutes.

Step 3

Read your story aloud to yourself or to someone in your inner circle. Turn off your internal editor and tell the story as you remember it. Then rehearse it until the story does not take longer than three minutes to tell, leaving out the parts of the story that are the most meaningful.

Step 4

Notice:

1. How does it feel telling your story?
2. What do you notice in your audience?
3. How does this impact you in how you lead, and why?

Chapter 5: Gauge your readiness for change

1. Reflection prompts your attitude towards change

Think of the last time you went through a big change, at work or in your personal life:

- What was your first reaction?
- What was your biggest concern?
- How did this change impact your mental well-being/ behaviour?
- Overall, how did it impact your professional/personal life?
- How did you communicate this change to others, if at all you did?
- What would you do differently (more of/less of)?

2. Test your agility when it comes to embracing change

According to Warner Burke, professor of psychology at Columbia University and developer of the Burke Learning Agility Inventory, leaders who successfully drive change possess a high degree of learning agility (in addition to EQ and Hope/ Optimism). Learning agility involves both cognitive and behavioural processes, and it involves how ready a leader is to:

- Seek out feedback
- Be curious and gather information about the system
- Take on risks and learn from failure
- Collaborate
- Reflect and learn
- Embrace swift (but not hasty) decision-making

Agility Quick test

Rate yourself on a scale of 1 (to a very small extent) to 5 (to a very great extent) to what extent you . . .

1. See feedback from others about your work performance.
2. Update your knowledge by collecting information from outside sources.

3. Discuss with others errors or mistakes you may have made and seek help in understanding what happened.
4. Put yourself in situations that involve a high degree of ambiguity about the process and/or outcome.
5. Facilitate learning from and among others.
6. Collect data to test and try out a new idea about and/or approach to work.
7. Take time after an event to consider what happened, why it happened that way and how things should be done moving forward.
8. Move easily between different ideas and perspectives.
9. Quickly pick up new information, ideas and behaviour.
10. Rely on using what has worked for you in the past.

Self-score here:

After you have rated yourself on each question, add up your total score for questions 1 to 9. For question 10, look at the scoring in reverse (i.e., if you rated yourself at 5, give yourself a 1; if you rated yourself at 4, give yourself 2; 3 stays the same) and then add this to your total score. Why? Question 10 tests our rigidity factor aka 'We have always done things this way', which is known to get in the way of agility.

If you score 40 or higher, then you may well be on your way to mastery. It's always good to practise some humility, though, as we know that for any self-rating assessment a remarkable 80 per cent of us tend to overrate ourselves. And if you are inspired to grow your change-agent muscles (as you know now, seeking feedback is a key component of learning agility), here is an experiment you may wish to try: why not have your team score you on the same questionnaire, and compare those results with your own?

Based on: Burke Learning Agility Inventory

Chapter 6: Manage difficult conversations

The Thomas-Kilmann framework

There are five basic conflict-handling modes: Collaboration, Accommodation, Competition, Avoidance and Compromise. Each of us can use all five modes. Most of us, however, have a 'preferred' conflict resolution style that corresponds with one of the five modes. However, all of these modes can be used effectively in the right situation. Before using any given mode, we need to ask ourselves:

1.   How important is the issue at hand?
2.   How important is the relationship to me?

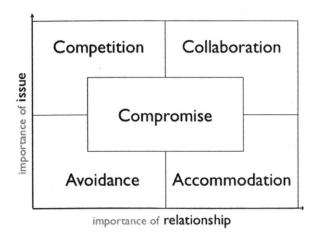

Source: https://kilmanndiagnostics.com/overview-thomas-kilmann-conflict-mode-instrument-tki/

3. Collaboration 'best practice'

Lesson 1: Stop thinking in positions of 'I versus you'

Our perception of conflict influences how we take our first step forward. We do not need to remain captive to childhood paradigms when it comes to conflict. While some of us are gifted, born mediators, navigating conflict can be learnt. Conflict is neither good nor bad. It is also not about winners and losers.

To shift beyond a 'fixed pie' mentality, we need to explore how we can expand the pie and negotiate. While it may not be feasible to get everything that we want, it is often possible to satisfy the majority of our interests.

In this light, when you enter a negotiation, consider what would be acceptable outcomes for you and rank them in order of preference. Also, have a Best Alternative to a Negotiated Agreement (BATNA) in place. What is your best course of action, should you and the other party not come to an agreement?

Lesson 2: Make it a choice

'Knowing when to fight is just as important as knowing how.'
—Terry Goodkind[1]

While some may argue that every conflict avoided is a lost opportunity, a good starting point is to gauge whether we really care about or need to engage with the other party. Unless you thrive on the adrenaline rush that comes with conflict, the time and energy involved in negotiation and the effects of this also need to be weighed against the benefits. Sometimes it is simply better to walk away.

Lesson 3: Keep your shades clear

Negotiations are often full of the unexpected and the complex. If you are not being clear about your own values, beliefs and emotional triggers, then chances are that your shades are dirty.

If we are not checking whether our assumptions about the reality are valid, then we risk stumbling in the dark when it comes to influencing others.

As you are getting ready to enter a specific negotiation, here are three questions to clarify for yourself:

> What outcome am I looking to achieve?
> What are some of my main concerns, going in?
> What needs am I ultimately trying to meet?

Also, take a moment to consider a time when you handled conflict well. Which of your strengths were particularly useful? Now, think of a time when you did not manage conflict constructively. What were the key emotional triggers that tended to trip you up in general? (Keep a list!) What needs are associated with these?

Lesson 4: Rehearse

You may remember the Hans Christian Andersen fairy tale, *The Emperor's New Clothes*, where the emperor's weavers claimed a new fabric was invisible to all who were 'hopelessly stupid'. No one, not even his advisers, dared tell the emperor that he was naked. One day, as the emperor strolled through the village, a boy in the crowd shouted out that the emperor was wearing nothing.

Who in your crowd is willing to shout out and hold you accountable? For tough negotiations, get an objective perspective from someone you trust and who gives you candid feedback. Consider role-playing to gauge how good your influencing skills really are.

Lesson 5: Lead with warmth

Many of my clients, in particular female executives, are reluctant to accommodate anything that looks like a compromise during negotiations: 'I don't want to be a doormat,' is a frequent pushback I receive as a coach. However, research confirms that leading with warmth, as we aspire to influence others, facilitates trust as it communicates that we are attentive to their needs.

Warmth expresses itself not only in what we say but also in how we say it. Vision is—hands down—our leading sense, taking up half of our brain's resources. It is not surprising, then, that body language heavily influences how other people think and feel about us and also how we feel about ourselves, as there is a feedback loop. Try smiling for a couple of minutes and your brain will increase its serotonin production, which is responsible for the feeling of happiness.

Suggest a time for your discussion that accommodates the other party's schedule. Consider using a more welcoming space in or outside the office. A 2010 study by MIT and Yale brain researchers confirms this. Offer the other party a comfortable chair and a coffee and they will be more flexible in their demands.

Add competence and a projection of strength to the mix, and you become a 'happy warrior'.

Lesson 6: Listen. Carefully.

Start any negotiation by inquiring about the other party's perspective first. Rather than delivering your version of the story and risking a defensive reaction, you are getting a general sense as to where they are coming from. Also, if you do this, they are more likely to listen to you when it's your turn to speak. Questions you may ask are:

> What is your goal or desired outcome?
> How important is this goal to you?
> What relationships are important to you?
> What are you most concerned about?

> What are some of the influencing factors that you might not be aware of?
> What are your specific needs and what outcomes would address those?

Some of the answers to these questions will be hard to simply listen to and not react. Remember that listening and looking for a place of mutual understanding do not mean you agree with the other person. This is a tough test of your listening skills. Powerful listening means you don't go into your own head. You fully concentrate on what the other person is saying—as well as on what they are not saying . . . Observation of their body language, facial expressions and tone of voice can give you good clues as to what they may care most about.

Bonus tip: As you are listening, in addition to open body language (Lesson 5), send verbal signals of acknowledgement, such as 'Okay, go on', 'uh huh' or 'tell me more'.

Lesson 7: Meet them where they are

As you are listening, show empathy where appropriate. 'I can imagine that this must have been hard/difficult/frustrating . . .' Dance in the moment, step to the side of your 'adversary' and let go of trying to control their reaction—you can't. If you perceive common ground, be sure to mention it—'It is clear that this is frustrating for both of us. So, moving forward, what is important to you now?'

Paraphrasing involves restating what someone has said using other words. It lets the other party know they have been heard. You validate their concerns. As you summarize milestones, do *not* say 'What you are trying to say is . . . ', but rather, start with, 'So, if I understand you correctly . . .' In other words, what you are saying is, 'Let me make sure I got this right . . .', or 'Do you mean that . . .?'

Paraphrasing can also serve as an opener to probe for more information: 'Can I ask a couple of questions?' Once you have listened to the other person, you have won yourself a hearing to assert your own needs.

Lesson 8: Stay calm . . . and carry on

It is particularly tough to manage emotional triggers when time constraints are factored into the equation. In response to requests such as 'I need it now!', consider asking 'What is important about having it now?' (And if it's you who puts on the pressure, ask yourself the same question.) This might allow you to address an underlying need differently.

Also, if you are someone who needs time for reflection before making a decision, buy additional time. Play back the conversation that has happened up to that point: 'To make sure I get what you are saying . . .' or, 'Hold on, let me make sure I get this right, can we back up for a minute and review how we got here . . .' You may also ask to enlist third party counsel or check in with the other parties who are involved prior to deciding.

If you're tempted to blow up in the face of antagonism, pause for a moment before you respond: count to three and take a couple of deep breaths. Or take a break, step out into the corridor, go for a walk. In short, remove yourself from the psychological pressure in the room. Imagine it's five years from now. What do you think you will have learnt from this conflict? How will you feel about how you handled it? What advice will the 'older you' tell the 'younger you' that is experiencing the challenge?

At all times, what helps you control your initial reaction is keeping your eyes on the prize: what is it that you really want as an outcome?

Tip: Ask yourself before saying something: 'Is it kind, is it relevant, is it true?' If the answer is 'no' for any of these, bite your lip and choose words that meet all these criteria.

Lesson 9: State your case. Tactfully.

Now it is time to share your perspective. Your goal is for people to understand your view without making them defensive. The more you can bring their defences down, the more you can get them to trust you, the more likely they are to be willing and able to hear you.

Own what is yours. Apologize for any wrongdoing on your part first. And, where there is room for doubt, consider stating it in a more unambiguous fashion, such as 'The information I got was that our client proposal came out as scheduled. I'll have to take a closer look into this.'

Be specific about what you need. Rather than playing the risky game of having others guess what you want, be direct and as succinct as you can. For example, 'I need you to say what the priorities for this project are.'

Attack the problem. Not the person. If the goal is to fix the problem, pointing fingers will cause the other party to check out and become defensive. One way to overcome this temptation is to focus on the future.

Lesson 10: Brainstorm and agree on 'what's next'

'We can't solve problems by using the same kind of thinking we used when we created them.'

—Albert Einstein[2]

You understand what the other party's needs are (in addition to your own). You have identified common ground. Now you are ready to develop acceptable solutions. Select those options that will work for both of you. 'Reality-test' them using the criteria of fairness and reciprocity to ensure that needs are met on both sides. Mention the other party's needs first; use the 'we' as well as the 'and' perspectives as you assert your own needs:

> 'If we move forward with this option, how can we make sure it addresses your need for abc and my need for xyz?'
> 'I know this is important for the two of us. You do need abc and I need xyz. What are the options that get us there?'
> 'What I heard you say is . . . and from my point of view what I need is . . . How can this option meet these criteria?'

If you are in a genuine deadlock, explore openly the costs of there being no agreement with the other party, holding up the mirror to what is at stake for the two of you. As a last resort, you may choose to let the other party know that you have a BATNA: 'I have other ideas on how to resolve this; however, my hope is that we resolve this together.' This tactic works best if none of the alternatives was acceptable. This is never to be used as a threat but as another piece of information.

Lesson +1: Celebrate agreement. Write it up.

Summarizing the main points of an agreement helps avoid future misunderstandings and sets standards of accountability. Sometimes a simple email to all the participants can do the job. Be sure to mention how and by when the solution will be implemented, and also the milestones and metrics.

APPENDIX 2

Recommended Reading

Chapter 1: From Ana's library

- *The Drama of the Gifted Child*, Alice Miller[1]
- *Trauma and Recovery*, Judith Herman[2]
- *The Leader on the Couch*, Manfred Kets de Vries[3]
- *Mindset: How You Can Fulfil Your Potential*, Carol Dweck[4]
- *The Psychology of Executive Coaching: Theory and Application*, Bruce Peltier[5]

Chapter 2: From Ana's library

- *Wired for Story*, Lisa Cron[6]
- *All Marketers Are Liars*, Seth Godin[7]
- *Made to Stick: Why Some Ideas Survive and Others Die*, Chip Heath and Dan Heath[8]
- *The Storytelling Animal*, Jonathan Gottschall[9]
- *Stories that Stick*, Kindra Hall[10]

(And as a bonus read: *The Beggar King and the Secret of Happiness*, Joel ben Izzy)[11]

Chapter 3: From Saurabh's library

- *Richer, Wiser, Happier: How the World's Greatest Investors Win in Markets and Life*, William Green[12]
- *Altered Traits*, Daniel Goleman and Richard Davidson[13]
- *The Folly of Fools: The Logic of Deceit and Self-Deception in Human Life*, Robert Trivers[14]
- *Zero to One*, Peter Thiel[15]
- *In an Uncertain World*, Robert Rubin[16]
- *Five Dysfunctions of a Team*, Patrick Lencioni[17]

Chapter 4: From Saurabh's library

- *Principles*, Ray Dalio[18]
- *Capital: The Story of Long-Term Investment Excellence*, Charles Ellis[19]
- *The Power Law*, Sebastian Mallaby[20]
- *The Power of Habit*, Charles Duhigg[21]
- *Daily Rituals: How Artists Work*, Mason Currey[22]
- *Mastery*, Robert Greene[23]
- *Range: How Generalists Triumph in a Specialized World*, David Epstein[24]
- *The Mind is Flat*, Nick Chater[25]

Chapter 5: From Ana's library

- *The Power of Habit*, Charles Duhigg[26]
- *What Got You Here Won't Get You There*, Marshall Goldsmith[27]
- *Switch: How to Change Things When Change is Hard*, Chip Heath and Dan Heath[28]
- *Immunity to Change*, Robert Kegan and Lisa Lahey[29]
- *Changing for Good*, James Prochaska[30]

From Saurabh's library

- *Influence: How and Why People Agree to Things*, Robert Cialdini[31]
- *Grit: The Power of Passion and Perseverance*, Angela Duckworth[32]
- *Leaders Eat Last*, Simon Sinek[33]
- *Quiet: The Power of Introverts in a World that Can't Stop Talking*, Susan Cain[34]
- *Loonshots: How to Nurture the Crazy Ideas That Win Wars, Cure Diseases, and Transform Industries*, Safi Bahcall[35]

Chapter 6: From Ana's library

- *Brain Rules: 12 Principles for Surviving and Thriving at Work, Home, and School*, John Medina[36]
- *Difficult Conversations: How to Discuss What Matters Most*, Douglas Stone, Bruce Patton and Sheila Heen[37]
- *Getting Past No*, William Ury[38]
- *Why Zebras Don't Get Ulcers*, Robert Sapolsky[39]
- *Psychology: Adventures in Perception and Personality*, Christian Jarrett and Joannah Ginsburg[40]

From Saurabh's library

- *Judgement Calls: Twelve Stories of Big Decisions and the Teams that Got It Right*, Thomas H. Davenport and Brooke Manville[41]
- *Ego is the Enemy: The Fight to Master Our Greatest Opponent*, Ryan Holiday[42]
- *The Art of Strategy*, Avinash Dixit and Barry J. Nalebuff[43]
- *Radical Uncertainty: Decision-Making for an Unknowable Future*, John Kay and Merwyn King[44]

- *Good Strategy/Bad Strategy: The Difference and Why It Matters*, Richard P. Rumelt[45]

Chapter 7: From Ana's library

- *Staring at the Sun,* Irvin Yalom[46]
- *Man's Search for Meaning,* Viktor Frankl[47]
- *Being Mortal,* Atul Gawande[48]
- *Flow,* Mihaly Csikszentmihalyi[49]
- *On Becoming a Person,* Carl Rogers[50]

From Saurabh's library

- *A Portrait of the Artist as a Young Man,* James Joyce[51]
- *Buffett: The Making of an American Capitalist,* Roger Lowenstein[52]
- *Shoe Dog: A Memoir by the Creator of Nike,* Phil Knight[53]
- *Start with Why,* Simon Sinek[54]
- *Wanting: The Power of Mimetic Desire in Everyday Life,* Luke Burgis[55]
- *India: A Million Mutinies Now,* V.S. Naipaul[56]

Thank You

gratitude

/ ɡrætəˌtud/

The quality of being thankful, readiness to show appreciation for and to return kindness

In positive psychology research, gratitude is consistently associated with well-being and health. Acknowledging the goodness in our lives—which is at least partially outside of ourselves—makes us more optimistic, boosts self-esteem, improves decision-making, increases resilience and makes us less likely to have aches and pains. To experience the benefits of gratitude we need to practise it regularly. This is our opportunity to take a moment and acknowledge all those who have contributed to our work and who have made this book possible.

In the spirit of radical transparency, this gratitude exercise also has its moments of angst when we think we might forget to mention one of our supporters, big or small. You know how it is. We therefore also thank all of you who are not specifically mentioned here by name. This one's for you.

The authors of this book would not have met had it not been for Egon Zehnder's Namrita Jhangiani and Vineet Hemrajani. We both owe them a big 'thank you' for facilitating our introduction, for trusting Ana's skill and experience, and thereby helping Saurabh quite literally start a new chapter in his life. In this context, Ana owes a thank you to David Noble and Saurabh to Alok Vajpeyi for connecting us to Namrita in the first place.

We wish to thank Ashok Wadhwa and Rahul Gupta for making this coaching engagement a reality. They engaged Ana to help Saurabh evolve and mature as a leader. Saurabh benefited greatly from watching Ashok and Rahul conduct themselves in high-pressure business situations and thanks them for their mentorship in what were, to date, the most difficult years of his career.

A number of friends and colleagues generously offered their time and suggestions, which significantly enriched our work. In particular, we wish to thank Anirudha Dutta, Pramod Gubbi, Anupam Gupta, Zara Karschay, Elizabeth McCourt, Rakshit Ranjan, Philip James Rose, Anke Thiele and Graham Ward.

For reviewing the book and endorsing our work, we are forever grateful to Marc Bitzer, Gurcharan Das, Matt Goldberg, Professor Manfred Kets de Vries, Vinati Saraf Mutreja, Apurva Purohit, Matt Reintjes, Paige Ross and Narotam Sekhsaria. A very special thank you goes to Bram Schot who took the time out of his busy schedule to endorse our work by writing the foreword.

Manish Kumar of Penguin Random House India was the proactive and energetic editor who understood the value of this collaborative endeavour that we had embarked on. He helped us fine-tune the book proposal and then navigate the book expertly through several rounds of editing. Unfailingly positive in the face of tricky situations and with a keen sense of how to present complex material in an easy-to-understand manner, we were lucky to have had him as a partner on this journey.

Kripa Raman and Ralph Rebello did an outstanding job of copy-editing the book and thereby making the final version look much better than the initial drafts that the authors produced. We are grateful to them for helping us make this book far more reader-friendly than it would have been without their expert input.

We also wish to thank our readers who have stuck with us and must have turned the pages to land on this one.

Ana's moment of gratitude

I owe special thanks to Annette Soehnlein, Kim Maczyewski and Dawid Konowalczuk—you kept me moving. And to Ingrid Hagemeister whose homemade ratatouille nourished body and soul in those dark European winter months. To my creative friend Cherie Aarts-Coley and one 'n'. Thank you also to photographer Emma Bailey, to Vittoria Addis and to Ian Mizon for the invaluable IT support.

My greatest appreciation is for the teachers and mentors I have had as part of working as a coach and therapist, in particular David Cotson, Carol Kauffman, Jean-Claude Noel, Chris Peterson and Richard Stewart. A heartfelt thank you also goes to all my former clients—you have shown me the way and taught me so much, which lets me be a better coach for clients yet to come.

I also want to appreciate my peers who change the lives of so many by living as an example and by empowering others for greatness. Many have become friends: Barbara Beyaz, Jennifer Bezoza, Victoria Bouix, Laurence Bridot, Claudia Danser, Veronique Doux, Hanneke Frese, Wolfgang Gattermeyer, Kari Ericksen, Karen Erickson, Lisa Gellert, Andreas Janz, Oriane Kets de Vries and the KDVI community, Lisa Kohn,

James Lamper, Glain Roberts McCabe, Robyn McLeod, Claire Pointing, Betina Rama, Anne Samyn, Khoi Tu and Hande Yasargil. And a big thank you also goes to the INSEAD community at large.

To all my friends and their unwavering support and care: Tehmina and Nadeem Baig, Donna Baker, Reto Candinas, Alice Cardini, Douglas Choo, Anna Cooklin, Peter Firnhaber, Angela Franchini, Dana Hawes-Davis, Evadnye Keith, Josefina Llavallol, Carolyn Mathews, Richard Murray-Bruce, Patricia Reese-Bouyer, Linda Samios, Maud Vimeux, Christiana Voskarides and Theo Yardley. A big shout-out also to the Kensington Terrace friends!

To my extended family, the Lüneburger tribe, who generously supported me during this time of writing this book. Most notably, Klaus and Palfi with their loving presence, my talented bonus sister-in-law Theresa Palfi, and cousin Anni Kluge with Helmut, Lena and Lütte who took care of Apple during my travels.

To my parents who instilled in me a love for people and discovery, two essential ingredients for doing good and doing well.

To Apple, my furry companion who never left my side and whose shameless requests for treats and cuddles continue to make me laugh.

To my sweet Liv for allowing me to lose my fear of becoming a parent, for embracing my imperfections, and for teaching me about unconditional love.

To my husband Christoph, a champion of this adventure from its start. Thank you for your love, your brilliant brain and your generosity. And for making Liv with me and for showing me that 'anything is possible'. It was you all along.

To my co-author Saurabh with more than I can ever say. This is a book I never thought could be written, as the very foundation of coaching is a confidential dialogue between two people behind closed doors. He is that client who had the courage to open that door. Co-authoring is also a complex process, one that can go horribly wrong. Instead, we have deepened our dialogues and grown our friendship. Your belief that we have something valuable to share was the inspiration for this book. And without your enthusiastic 'Let's do it', it would not have happened.

Saurabh's moment of gratitude

When Sarbani and I arrived in India fifteen years ago as young, inexperienced parents and I took charge of a loss-making company in a country in which I had never worked before, my mental circuits were maxed out. Dr Sharmila Banwat provided invaluable guidance and many hours of patient counselling in those difficult years. I am very grateful to Dr Banwat for not only helping me stay sane through these years but also for inculcating in me a love for reading about how the mind works and how the human brain processes emotions and information.

The fact that I found the time and the mental space to collaborate with Ana on this book is in large part due to the tremendous work done by the team at Marcellus Investment Managers. This team has, in the space of four years, helped build a market-leading alternative investment management business in India. Every single member of Marcellus's 120-strong team has stood up and made a difference through the turmoil of COVID-19 and its chaotic aftermath. I owe a particular debt of gratitude to Sudhanshu Nahta, Manish Hemnani, Ashvin Shetty, Nitesh Bhadani, Salil Desai, Tej Shah, Parimal Deuskar and Sapana Bhavsar.

My parents, Chaitali and Prasanta, helped Ana understand how they raised me and my sister, Panchali. The upbringing they gave me resulted in my love for reading and learning, which resulted in me first becoming a bibliophile and then a prolific author. I would like to thank Maa and Baba for helping me understand that a life lived in the pursuit of money is not a life worth living.

Young Saisriyaa Patro volunteered to read all of my previous books and identify in them common strands of thought. Saisriyaa's research helped me understand my own work better. That, in turn, helped me structure Chapter 4 of the book around a few salient themes that have characterized my career.

Sarbani and I have known each other since primary school and without Sarbani's unconditional love and support, I would not be where I am today. She motivates me to grow as a parent and as a husband. And it is Sarbani who makes me want to become a more balanced, better person in the years to come.

Finally, I would like to thank Ana for agreeing to work on this unique time-consuming collaborative project despite the many calls on her time and despite her initial misgivings about becoming an author. Given Ana's evident flair for writing, I hope this is the first of many books that Ana will author so that the world at large can benefit from her wisdom and her expertise.

Courtesy: Fox meets Owl Ltd

Notes

Chapter 1: Spilling the Beans

1. Irvin Yalom, Ginny Elkin, *Every Day Gets a Little Closer: A Twice-Told Therapy*, Basic Books, 1974.
2. The Galleria dell'Accademia di Firenze is one of Italy's most visited art museums and is located in Florence, Italy. Most of the works shown here are from the period 1300–1600, and it is famous for having Michelangelo's sculpture *David* in its collection.
3. The International Coaching Federation (ICF), considered by many in the industry to be the gold standard institution for coaches, defines coaching in a similar way, as 'partnering with clients in a thought-provoking and creative process that inspires them to maximize their personal and professional potential. The process of coaching often unlocks previously untapped sources of imagination, productivity and leadership'.
4. Jonah Lehrer, *How We Decide,* Houghton Mifflin Harcourt, 2009.
5. ICF Global Coaching Study, 2020.
6. Scott D. Miller, Barry L. Duncan, Mark A. Hubble, *Escape from Babel: Toward a Unifying Language for Psychotherapy Practice*, Norton, 1997.
7. https://coachingfederation.org/app/uploads/2021/03/March2021_FactSheet.pdf
8. Adam Grant, *Give and Take: A Revolutionary Approach to Success*, Weidenfeld & Nicholson, 2013.
9. The majority of coaches are 50+, but younger coaches are on the rise (ICF Global Coaching Study, 2020).

10. To learn more about the Hogan: https://www.hoganassessments. com/assessment/hogan-personality-inventory/
11. Diane Coutu, Carol Kauffman, 'What Can Coaches Do for You?' *Harvard Business Review*, 2009.
12. Atul Gawande, 'Personal Best', *The New Yorker*, 2011.
13. Ernesto Spinelli, *Tales of Un-knowing: Therapeutic Encounters from an Existential Perspective*, Duckworth, 1997.
14. Scott D. Miller, Barry L. Duncan, Mark A. Hubble, *Escape from Babel*.
15. Name and facts altered to protect client confidentiality.
16. Eric Schmidt III, *Trillion Dollar Coach*, HarperCollins, 2019.
17. Dr Paul Brand, Philip Yancey, *The Gift of Pain*, Zondervan, 1993.
18. David H. Maister, Charles H. Green, *The Trusted Advisor*, Free Press, 2000. To assess your trustworthiness and how you can improve it, visit http://trustedadvisor.com/
19. ICF Coaching Report 2020.
20. Walter Kiechel III, *The Lords of Strategy*, Harvard Business Press, 2010, note 5 to chapter 14, p. 330.
21. Diane Coutu, Carol Kauffman, 'What Can Coaches Do for You?'.
22. Name changed to protect client confidentiality.
23. A philosophy of bottom-up leadership is generally where leaders 'serve' their people. Beyond providing direction and motivation with an eye on the bottom line, a servant leader also ensures that followers develop in a broader sense—in their career, knowledge and strengths as well as in their mental and physical well-being.
24. Terry R. Bacon, *Measuring the Effectiveness of Executive Coaching*, Korn Ferry Institute, 2011.
25. See Chapter 5.
26. Ashley Stahl, 'This New Year's Set Goals, Not Resolutions', *Forbes*, 2021. Source: https://www.forbes.com/sites/ashleystahl/2021/12/09/this-new-years-set-goals-not-resolutions/
27. To learn about your own strengths profile, visit https://viacharacter.org/
28. As retold over dinner many years ago by Gabriel Sánchez Zinny, who led the internal professional development efforts at Egon Zehnder in addition to his executive search role as a partner for the firm. By the way, the eastern grey squirrel runs at a speed of 32 km/h, while turkeys run at about 40 km/h (and fly at 90 km/h).

29. For more on how to use different signature strengths, see Chapter 5.

Chapter 2: In a Nutshell: The Coach's Perspective

1. More here: https://www.viacharacter.org/about
2. Robert Kegan, Lisa Lahey, 'The Real Reason People Won't Change', *Harvard Business Review*, 2001.
3. Efficiency and effectiveness are different. Whereas efficiency is the ability to achieve a goal with the minimum amount of money, time and effort spent, effectiveness is the degree to which a person is successful in delivering or achieving a desired outcome.
4. Culture Map Dimensions
   Cross-cultural leadership expert Professor Erin Meyer at INSEAD has, based on extensive research, developed eight dimensions as it relates to cognitive, relational and behavioural similarities and differences between cultures.
   Dimension 1: Low context (explicit) vs High context (implied) communication
   Dimension 2: Direct negative feedback vs Indirect negative feedback
   Dimension 3: Egalitarian vs Hierarchical leadership
   Dimension 4: Consensus vs Top-down decision-making
   Dimension 5: Task-based vs Relationship-based trust
   Dimension 6: Confrontational vs Avoids confrontation
   Dimension 7: Linear-time vs Flexible-time scheduling
   Dimension 8: Principles (concepts, theory) first vs Application (facts) first persuasion

Chapter 3: In a Nutshell: The Client's Perspective

1. Saurabh Mukherjea, *Syndicated Lending in Emerging Markets*, Euromoney Books, 1999.
2. Teresa M. Amabile and Steven J. Kramer, 'The Power of Small Wins', *Harvard Business Review*, May 2011.
3. Rosie Ifould, '"Would you be willing?": Words to Turn a Conversation Around (And Those to Avoid)', *The Guardian*, 2017.

246   Notes

4. Saurabh Mukherjea, Anupam Gupta, *The Victory Project: Six Steps to Peak Potential*, Penguin Random House, 2020.
5. Robert Louis Stevenson, *The Strange Case of Dr Jekyll and Mr Hyde*, Longmans Green & Co, 1886.
6. Mihir Desai, *The Wisdom of Finance: Discovering Humanity in the World of Risk and Return*, Profile Books, 2018.
7. René Girard, Jean-Michel Oughourlian, Guy Lefort, Stephen Bann and Michael Leigh Metteer, *Things Hidden since the Foundation of the World*, Stanford University Press, 1978.
8. A character in the Hollywood movie *Wall Street* (1987), played by Michael Douglas.
9. Chris Wright, *No More Worlds to Conquer*, The Friday Project, 2016.
10. William Ernest Henley, *A Book of Verses*, David Nutt, 1888.
11. David Remnick, *King of the World: Muhammad Ali and the Rise of an American Hero*, Random House, 1998.

Chapter 4: A Leader's Hard-Won Lessons

1. Saurabh Mukherjea, Anupam Gupta, *The Victory Project: Six Steps to Peak Potential*, Penguin Random House, 2020.
2. Robert Greene, *Mastery*, Profile Books, 2012.
3. Yuval Noah Harari, *Sapiens: A Brief History of Humankind*, Penguin Random House, 2011.
4. Jack Welch, John A. Byrne, *Jack: Straight from the Gut*, Warner Books, 2001.
5. Lee Iacocca, *Iacocca: An Autobiography*, Bantam Dell Pub Books, 1984.
6. Louis V. Gerstner, *Who Says Elephants Can't Dance?*, HarperCollins, 2002.
7. Ray Dalio, *Principles*, Simon and Schuster, 2017.
8. Charles Duhigg, *The Power of Habit: Why We Do What We Do in Life and in Business*, Random House, 2012.
9. To quote Duhigg: 'Most of the choices we make each day may feel like the products of well-considered decision making but they're not. They are habits. And though each habit means relatively little on its own, over time the meals we order, what we say to our kids each night . . . have enormous impacts on our health . . . and happiness.

One paper published by a Duke University researcher in 2006 found that more than 40 per cent of the actions people performed each day weren't actual decisions, but habits . . .

'When you dream up a new invention . . . it's the outside parts of your brain at work. That's where the most complex thinking occurs. Deeper inside the brain and closer to . . . where the brain meets the spinal column, are older, more primitive structures. They control our automatic behaviours, such as breathing and swallowing . . . Towards the centre of the skull is a golf ball-sized lump of tissue that is similar to what you might find inside the head of a fish, reptile or mammal. This is the basal ganglia . . . [Scientists have found that] basal ganglia was central to recalling patterns and acting on them. The basal ganglia, in other words, stored habits even while the rest of the brain went to sleep.' [square brackets are ours]

Chapter 5: Do We Ever Arrive?

1. A philosopher from the ancient Greek city of Ephesus. He belongs to the pre-Socratic era.
2. Check the annual Coaching Colloquium by the European School of Management (ESMT), where together with colleagues, we shared (anonymized) client cases, discussed projects and explored best-practice coaching approaches.
3. As coaches, I believe we must be open to the idea that when we over-attribute a client's positive change results to our own efforts, we may have fallen prey to a moment of 'grandiose narcissism', where we think we are almighty. The opposite is true as well: if we believe that a client's failure to change is due to our failure to deliver, we may be thinking narcissistic thoughts, in that we believe we are omnipotent and that it is up to us for clients to change.
4. For more, see viacharacter.org
5. Movie popcorn can teach us something about shaping paths and the importance of paying attention to the environment of a leader to support their change agenda. A 2016 study led by Cornell University showed that audiences tend to eat more when a main character in the film keeps on eating. Equally, they were more ready to stop if the actors finished eating. Some large popcorn bags reportedly

contain up to 1800 calories—more than the entire recommended daily allowance for a school-age child. Coming back to change, by shaping a situation, by enlisting the support of key stakeholders in the organization, coaches can help leaders strengthen their resolve to change their behaviour, and we see better results.

6. As a side note, it is always a good idea to reference. This is also of relevance in the search for the right coach. A coach's former clients are a valuable source for quality control. While this has rarely happened with me personally, on occasion, potential clients have asked to speak with previous clients. This form of referencing allows the inquiring leader to ask some probing questions and gain greater clarity on how to move forward. However, the challenge here is, of course, that it is the coach who pre-selects the references, and they will unlikely include any disgruntled clients. The most effective references, therefore, are independent rather than nominated by the coach.

7. C. Peterson, 'The Future of Optimism', *American Psychologist*, 55, 2000, pp. 44–55. We also know that hope and an optimistic explanatory style can be cultivated through psychotherapy, leading to raised levels of resilience and well-being.

8. C. Peterson, M. Seligman, *Character Strengths and Virtues*, Oxford Press, 2004.

9. I try to not cyber-stalk my clients, but when I 'googled' Saurabh, here it was: Saurabh in 2022 was announced by the Indian media as one of the Leaders of Tomorrow. His followership is significant by now. You can also read up on Saurabh on Wikipedia, CNBC and other media outlets. He is not only seen as a visionary but also as a premier investor. As one of his fans posted, 'If you want to sustain in the market and accumulate your wealth, simply follow his stocks.'

10. S. Oishi, E. Diener, R.E. Lucas, 'The Optimal Level of Well-Being. Can We Be Too Happy?' *Perspectives on Psychological Science*, 2, 2007, pp. 346–360.

11. As a side note, some of his 2017 strengths, such as Love of Learning (from rank #1 to #10), continue to have a strong presence, despite being overtaken by new strengths Saurabh has worked to add.

12. This large cultural group is also known for its immersion in the arts, literature, politics, military, science and technology. In essence, they

excel in leadership and knowledge, much of what Saurabh has been praised for in any feedback that I received on him.

13. Chris Peterson and Martin Seligman in their book *Character Strengths and Virtues, A Handbook and Classification* define transcendence strengths as those that are connected to the universe and provide meaning. These strengths include gratitude, appreciation of beauty and excellence, humour, hope and spirituality.

14. You may have heard of the Yerkes-Dodson Law where, in 1908, two Harvard researchers captured the relationship between stress and performance in a simple bell curve. More here: https://en.wikipedia.org/wiki/Yerkes%E2%80%93Dodson_law

15. Francesca Gina, 'Are You Too Stressed to Be Productive? Or Not Stressed Enough', *HBR*, 2016.

16. Alice Miller, Ruth Ward, *The Drama of the Gifted Child*, Basic Books, 1997.

17. R. Kegan, L. Lahey, *Immunity to Change*, Harvard Business School Publishing Corporation, 2009. It is the 'one foot on the gas, one foot on the brake' syndrome that Bob Kegan and Lisa Lahey have researched extensively. Sometimes it need not go all the way back to childhood, but very often that is where we need to begin.

18. Source: https://www.azlyrics.com/lyrics/direstraits/thebug.html

19. S.R. Covey, *The 7 Habits of Highly Effective People*, Simon and Schuster, 2020.

Chapter 6: In Session: A Coaching Conversation

1. 'Fishbowl' is a strategy for creating learning opportunities. In the inner circle, or fishbowl, a discussion takes place between coach and client. 'Students' in the outer circle listen to the discussion and take notes. It can be an extremely useful way of teaching skills and engaging the learner.

2. It would be another book if we were to include the full-length conversations!

3. Research in attachment theory shows that we tend to repeat 80 per cent of what we experience as children with our own offspring (or we do exactly the opposite, not usually a better solution either). A bit

cheekily, Philip Larkin's poem 'This be the Verse' from the book *High Windows*, Faber and Faber, 1974, comes to mind:

They fuck you up, your mum and dad.
    They may not mean to, but they do.
They fill you with the faults they had
    And add some extra, just for you.

But they were fucked up in their turn
    By fools in old-style hats and coats,
Who half the time were soppy-stern
    And half at one another's throats.

Man hands on misery to man.
    It deepens like a coastal shelf.
Get out as early as you can,
    And don't have any kids yourself.

4. Source: https://hbr.org/2018/09/the-business-case-for-curiosity
5. This model is based on two dimensions of conflict management: assertiveness and empathy. Based on these two dimensions, there are five conflict-resolution strategies: Competing, Avoiding, Accommodating, Collaborating and Compromising. The idea is to help Saurabh develop a greater repertoire when it comes to responding to others.
6. Phenomenology is a form of exploration that focuses on a client's lived experience within the world, in this case, the coaching experience and space. As a client experiences the coaching space, he or she is encouraged to make sense of what is happening.
7. The Thomas-Kilmann model of conflict resolution (refer to the resources at the end of this book).
8. A brief narrative on amygdala hijacks. When we experience an amygdala hijack, the emotional part of the brain—the amygdala—overrides the thinking part of the brain—the neocortex—in response to a perceived threat. Depending on the degree of hijack, our ability to reason and to think logically is compromised. Your working memory will become less efficient and your blood pressure, adrenaline and hormone levels rise. It can take three to four hours for the hijack effects to clear the system. While an overactive amygdala serves a

useful purpose when faced with a genuine physical threat (when emotions and reactions are crucial), it can cause problems when the threat is emotional. During the hijack, the number of options you can perceive will decrease dramatically. Instead of maybe four ways of resolving a problem, we may only perceive three, then two (an either/or choice), and then only one. When there is only one option left, the hijack is complete. We will turn to default, habitual behaviours; we are on autopilot and liable to make dangerously biased decisions, and we lose our ability to communicate effectively. Successful leaders must know how to bypass the amygdala hijack, and gaining time and space away from a trigger is an excellent tactic.

Chapter 7: Stay Curious, My Friends

1.   Joseph B. Soloveitchik, *Lonely Man of Faith*, Doubleday, 1965.
2.   Barry Lopez, *Of Wolves and Men*, Charles Scribner's Sons, 1978, p. 284. 'To allow mystery, which is to say to yourself, "There could be more, there could be things we don't understand," is not to damn knowledge. It is to take a wider view. It is to permit yourself an extraordinary freedom: someone else does not have to be wrong in order that you may be right.'
3.   For more details, watch this terrific TED Talk from Zimbardo titled 'The Psychology of Time': Source: https://www.youtube.com/watch?v=bo4HiVetBd0
4.   Source: www.thetimeparadox.com
5.   Gin and tonic was created in India two centuries ago and is now enjoyed by happy drinkers the world over.

Appendix 1: Resources and Exercises

1.   Terry Goodkind, *The Faith of the Fallen*, Orion, 2000.
2.   Possibly a paraphrasing of Einstein's quote, 'A new type of thinking is essential if mankind is to survive and move toward higher levels', from 'Atomic Education Urged by Einstein', *New York Times*, 25 May 1946).

Appendix 2: Recommended Reading

1. Alice Miller, Ruth V. Ward, *The Drama of the Gifted Child: The Search for the True Self,* Harper Perennial, 1981.
2. Judith Lewis Herman, *Trauma and Recovery,* Basic Books, 1992.
3. Manfred F.R. Kets de Vries, *The Leader on the Couch: A Clinical Approach to Changing People and Organizations,* Jossey Books, 2006.
4. Carol S. Dweck, *Mindset: The New Psychology of Success,* Random House, 2006.
5. Bruce Peltier, *The Psychology of Executive Coaching: Theory and Application,* Brunner-Routledge, 2001.
6. Lisa Cron, *Wired for Story: The Writer's Guide to Using Brain Science to Hook Readers from the Very First Sentence,* Ten Speed Press, 2011.
7. Seth Godin, *All Marketers are Liars: The Underground Classic That Explains How Marketing Really Works – And Why Authenticity Is the Best Marketing of All,* Portfolio, 2005.
8. Chip Heath and Dan Heath, *Made to Stick: Why Some Ideas Take Hold and Some Come Unstuck,* Belhaven Press, 2007.
9. Jonathan Gottschall, *The Storytelling Animal: How Stories Make Us Human,* Houghton Mifflin Harcourt, 2012.
10. Kindra Hall, *Stories that Stick: How Storytelling Can Captivate Customers, Influence Audiences, and Transform Your Business,* HarperCollins Leadership, 2019.
11. Joel ben Izzy, *The Beggar King and The Secret of Happiness: A True Story,* Workman Publishing, 2005.
12. William Green, *Richer, Wiser, Happier: How the World's Greatest Investors Win in Markets and Life,* Scribner, 2021.
13. Daniel Goleman, Richard J Davidson, *Altered Traits: Science Reveals How Meditation Changes Your Mind, Brain, and Body,* Avery, 2017.
14. Robert Trivers, *The Folly of Fools: The Logic of Deceit and Self-Deception in Human Life,* Basic Books, 2011.
15. Peter Thiel, *Zero to One,* Currency, 2014.
16. Robert Edward Rubin, Jacob Weisberg, *In an Uncertain World: Tough Choices from Wall Street to Washington,* Random House, 2003.
17. Patrick Lencioni, Charles Stransky, *The Five Dysfunctions of a Team,* Penguin Random House, 2002.
18. Ray Dalio, *Principles,* Simon and Schuster, 2017.

19. Charles Ellis, *Capital: The Story of Long-Term Investment Excellence*, Wiley, 2004.
20. Sebastian Mallaby, *The Power Law*, Penguin, 2022.
21. Charles Duhigg, *The Power of Habit: Why We Do What We Do in Life and in Business*, Random House, 2012.
22. Mason A. Currey, *Daily Rituals: How Artists Work*, Alfred A. Knopf, 2013.
23. Robert Greene, *Mastery*, Profile Books, 2012.
24. David Epstein, *Range: How Generalists Triumph in a Specialized World*, Macmillan, 2019.
25. Nick Chater, *The Mind is Flat: The Illusion of Mental Depth and the Improvised Mind*, Penguin Books, 2019.
26. Charles Duhigg, *The Power of Habit: Why We Do What We Do in Life and in Business*.
27. Marshall Goldsmith, Mark Reiter, *What Got You Here Won't Get You There: How Successful People Become Even More Successful!*, Hyperion, 2007.
28. Chip Heath, Dan Heath, *Switch: How to Change Things When Change is Hard*, Broadway Books, 2005.
29. Robert Kegan, Lisa Laskow Lahey, *Immunity to Change*, Harvard Business Press, 2009.
30. James O. Prochaska, John C. Norcross, Carlo C. DiClemente, *Changing for Good*, Ontario Quill Press, 2002.
31. Robert Cialdini, *Influence: How and Why People Agree to Things*, Quill, 1984.
32. Angela Duckworth, *Grit: The Power of Passion and Perseverance*, Scribner, 2016.
33. Simon Sinek, *Leaders Eat Last: Why Some Teams Pull Together and Some Don't*, Portfolio Penguin, 2013.
34. Susan Cain: *Quiet: The Power of Introverts in a World that Can't Stop Talking*, Penguin, 2013.
35. Safi Bahcall, *Loonshots: How to Nurture the Crazy Ideas That Win Wars, Cure Diseases, and Transform Industries*, St. Martin's Press, 2019.
36. John Medina, *Brain Rules: 12 Principles for Surviving and Thriving at Work, Home, and School*, Pear Press, 2008.

37. Douglas Stone, Bruce Patton, Sheila Heen, *Difficult Conversations: How to Discuss What Matters Most*, Penguin, 2010.
38. William Ury, *Getting Past No*, Bantam Books, 1993.
39. Robert Sapolsky, *Why Zebras Don't Get Ulcers*, St. Martin's Press, 2004.
40. Christian Jarrett, Joannah Ginsburg, *Psychology: Adventures in Perception and Personality*, Metro Books, 2014.
41. Thomas H. Davenport, Brooke Manville, *Judgement Calls: Twelve Stories of Big Decisions and the Teams that Got it Right*, Harvard Business Review Press, 2012.
42. Ryan Holiday, *Ego is the Enemy: The Fight to Master Our Greatest Opponent*, Profile Books, 2016.
43. Avinash Dixit, Barry J. Nalebuff, *The Art of Strategy*, W.W. Norton & Company, 2008.
44. John Kay, Merwyn King, *Radical Uncertainty: Decision-making for an Unknowable Future*, W.W. Norton & Company, 2020.
45. Richard P. Rumelt, *Good Strategy/Bad Strategy: The Difference and Why It Matters*, Profile, 2011.
46. Irvin Yalom, *Staring at the Sun*, Scribe Publications, 2008.
47. Viktor Frankl, *Man's Search for Meaning*, Verlag Für Jugend und Volk, 1946.
48. Atul Gawande, *Being Mortal*, Metropolitan Books, 2014.
49. Mihaly Csikszentmihalyi, *Flow*, Rider, 1992.
50. Carl Rogers, *On Becoming a Person*, Houghton Mifflin, 1961.
51. James Joyce, *A Portrait of the Artist as a Young Man*, B.W. Hubesch, 1916.
52. Roger Lowenstein, *Buffett: The Making of an American Capitalist*, Random House, 1995.
53. Phil Knight, *Shoe Dog: A Memoir by the Creator of Nike*, Simon and Schuster, 2016.
54. Simon Sinek, *Start with Why*, Portfolio/Penguin, 2009.
55. Luke Burgis, *Wanting: The Power of Mimetic Desire in Everyday Life*, St. Martin's Press, 2021.
56. V.S. Naipaul, *A Million Mutinies Now*, Heinemann, 1990.